Trial & Error

Tales of Well Meaning Political Decisions Gone Wrong

Jeff L. Schuster

ISBN:
ISBN-13: 978-1499553499
ISBN-10: 1499553498

DEDICATION

This book is dedicated to all of those who have desired a more civil and effective democratic political process.

CONTENTS

Preface

I believe that the United States is at a crossroads of political discourse. Most people do not readily understand the economic fallout of political decisions. Furthermore, it seems as if political decisions made by voters and politicians have more to do with personal scandals and innuendo rather than the substance of logical decisions. Our electorate right now is so polarized that we call each other names and never get down to the business of running our country. Family and friends refuse to talk about important political topics because they will somehow upset or offend others that disagree with their position. This reluctance leads to isolated political grumbling rather than genuine political progress.

When I watch the political discourse in our country, it pains me to see that our government officials and their supporters have devolved into discussions about things that really don't matter when determining our fate. We have government shutdowns, obstinate politicians on both sides and voters who are not fully educated on the issues or the consequences of political decisions. I truly believe that the United States and select local governments are in major jeopardy if we do not start making progress on decisions that need to be made and stop the petty bickering.

Trial & Error is a collection of several short stories told from the perspective of a Mayor that we would all probably love as a political leader even if his ideas do not always work out. I am a lover of a great story and felt like communicating political concepts through stories would be the optimum way to connect with those who may be jaded by other philosophical books on politics.

I hope that this book helps you understand the full impact of political decisions that seem quite harmless on the surface. Most of these decisions initially seem to offer untold benefits but end in catastrophic results to our economy and our social wellbeing. I hope that reading this book helps you gain a better understanding of the results of these decisions and why they lead to adverse results that may not be expected on the front end.

I believe you will find Mayor Wallaby to be fair in many of his decisions. At the end of each story about Mayor Wallaby and Trial Town, I have included a section that describes a real-world experience that mimics the lessons learned in Trial Town.

Most of all, I hope that this book informs you about the serious implications of key political issues and give you courage to cast a vote that makes a positive difference in our government's future.

INTRODUCTION TO TRIAL TOWN

Hi, my name is Arthur Wallaby. I'm the mayor of Trial Town. I want to tell you a brief story of how Trial Town came to be.

Recently, the President of the United States and a group of congressional representatives felt frustrated that many initiatives they tried in the federal government would end in larger debts and not really solve any of their problems. So they decided to pass a law to name Trial Town, an already established city of 100,000 people, as a test city. A test city means that we have been given special license by our citizens and by the Federal Government of the United States to test any form of government or economy. We are separated from any federal or state government and we can issue any laws that we like. The only requirement we have from the federal government is that we need to track any successes and/or failures so that US Government can learn from our mistakes and our successes.

Trial Town is located near the east coast in a secret location within the United States. We have a distant neighbor, Capital City, which may be mentioned from time to time; otherwise, we are a relatively isolated city. We have the typical city amenities like grocery stores, big-box stores, department stores, a post office, malls, a city hall, police stations, fire stations, parks, recreation centers, movie theatres, public schools, colleges, factories and a robust farming and ranching industry. Trial Town is a self-sustaining city. We do import and export with other countries, but we are able to manufacture many of the products that we use in our city. We even have our own military, intelligence organizations, border patrol and other departments that you may only find in a federal government.

I am the mayor of Trial Town. The great thing about Trial Town is that when our government policies fail, we get to clean the slate and start from the same place we were before we made the changes that caused the problems. That's right… Trial Town can build up massive debt or deplorable conditions for our citizens and with the press of a 'reset button', we turn the clock back; the bank accounts go back to their original balances and all of the damage that we have created with whatever government program we implement is reversed.

Unfortunately, you folks in the real world do not have our magic reset button. So you may recognize some long-term negative impacts when government leaders make the wrong decisions. I do hope that you will learn from our mistakes and some of our successes to make better decisions within your government.

1 PARTY POLITICS

"When politicians start talking about large groups of their fellow Americans as 'enemies,' it's time for a quiet stir of alertness. Polarizing people is a good way to win an election, and also a good way to wreck a country."
— Molly Ivins

In Trial Town, we have always had a traditional form of democracy. I am the mayor of Trial Town and we have a group of six folks who make up my city council; seven if you include me. Every two years the citizens of Trial Town elect or re-elect their mayor and members of city council. There are usually four candidates running for each position and the candidate with the most votes is elected. Many times the person with the most votes has received only 30% of all votes, meaning that the winning candidate really is supported by a minority of Trial Town's population.

I realized that Capital City did not have this problem and their winning candidates normally had the majority of voters' support when elected to office. I decided to have lunch with Capital City's mayor Don Westland to discuss what they were doing right.

We met at one of Mayor Westland's favorite spots in Capital City called the Main Street Café. After we dispensed with the traditional introductions and small talk, I decided to break the ice on the election discussion.

"Don," I said, "we seem to have a problem in Trial Town with our elections. We have four candidates running for one position and winners normally receive only 30% of the vote."

Mayor Westland interrupted. "That's a low percentage to support an elected official."

"That's what I wanted to talk to you about," I responded.

"Arthur, how can I help?"

"Don, it seems a large majority of voters support your winning candidates. I've heard rumors that winning candidates in Capital City get 55% of the vote. I was wondering if you could tell me your secret."

Don smiled. "Arthur, in Capital City we have a two-party system. Each party nominates a single candidate to represent their party in the election. That means we have only two candidates running for each position. In order to win, a candidate has to win more than 50% of the vote."

"This two-party system sounds like a simple solution. How do we get this system started in Trial Town?"

Don responded, "It's simple, Arthur. You simply establish a two-party election system in your City Charter and then allow the parties to establish their own platforms so that your voters can decide which party they'd like to belong to."

I left our lunch meeting with a new sense of purpose. This two-party system was a brilliant and simple concept that I knew would work well for Trial Town. It was a way to make sure that each elected official in our government would be supported by a majority of voters instead of the meager 30% support that all of us elected officials received.

I introduced the concept to my city council members and they were eager to participate in forming our new two-party system. The first party was called the Green Party and the second the Red Party. We created an election registration system where citizens of Trial Town could register as either a Green Party or Red Party member. We decided to have primary elections just like Capital City. Each party would decide which candidate they wanted to participate in the final election. This way there would only be two candidates running in the final election. The cost of this system would be slightly more as there would be two elections but it seemed well worth it to get majority support behind the winning candidate.

We announced this idea to the citizens of Trial Town and they were very happy with this two-party system. In fact, citizens started registering immediately with their desired party. People organized their parties and established belief platforms that they would stand for.

The Green Party established the following platform principles:

1) Treat all races, religious, and ethnic people equally;
2) Oppose any war unless the threat was a direct threat to Trial Town;
3) Support government programs that help the less fortunate; and
4) Public education must be available to all in Trial Town.

The Red Party established the following platform principles:

1) Financial responsibility is key to any successful government;
2) Religious and speech freedoms are paramount to a free society;
3) Support any war that would protect Trial Town's freedom; and
4) Strict enforcement of laws is the cornerstone of an organized society.

As I read both platforms, I felt so proud of each party. I would be honored to belong to either of them. Even though I saw little difference between them, most citizens of Trial Town were quick to sign up to either the Reds or the Greens. They then started holding party meetings they called caucuses, where they discussed their party's vision and which candidates best fit their party's platform standards. They also held fundraisers to raise money for their candidate's election campaign. I was amazed at how much money these political parties raised. By the time our first primary election rolled around, each party had amassed $1 million each for six city council member positions. In their speeches in the primary elections, each candidate would talk about how they would be better than the opposing candidate to represent their party's platform in the upcoming general election.

We had successful primary elections, with many party candidates being supported by about 30% of their party's vote. Then the commotion really started. There were twelve candidates for six city council seats. I had never seen such an intense election in all my days as mayor of Trial Town. There were flyers all over the place and non-stop TV and radio advertisements. Candidates were making speeches at decked-out halls, trying to win as many votes as they could. The other thing I noticed about this election, which did not happen in past elections, was the mudslinging. Candidates and their parties were making their opposing candidates and parties out to be pure evil. I also heard very few substantive discussions about the issues that would face our city in the very near future. Each candidate had to tip the scale their direction and they would win. The intensity was something else.

Just to get a taste of the environment, I attended one of the debates between Paul Fredrick, a Red Party candidate, and Jim Peck, the Green Party candidate.

The moderator Peggy Stanton from Channel 7 News started the debate, "We're pleased to host one of the most prolific debates of Trial Town's first two-party final election between Paul Fredrick, the Red Party candidate, and Jim Peck, the Green Party candidate. I'll pose a question to a specific candidate. This candidate will have exactly one minute to respond to the question. The opposing candidate will then have one minute to respond to the same question. I ask the audience to remain silent during the debate. We'll be televising this debate live with no interruptions for commercials."

Each candidate had their own podium with their party logo and both were dressed in their best suit and tie. They looked quite professional. Naturally, Paul Fredrick wore a red tie while Jim Peck wore a green tie. The moderator, Peggy Stanton, was seated in front of the audience, facing both candidates. Two TV cameras were stationed on both sides of the stage to pan on the left or right candidate and the moderator. I was very excited to see the show.

Peggy began with her first question. "Mr. Fredrick, you've stated that Trial Town spends too much money. What spending programs would you cut from Trial Town's current services?"

Paul Fredrick cleared his throat. "Peggy, I want to first thank Channel 7 and you for hosting this debate and thank our studio audience, who has taken the time to be engaged in our election process. As you know, Trial Town has spent money frivolously on many programs that don't benefit anyone in our town. I can't name a specific program that I'd cut until I undertake a dialogue with our mayor and other members of the city council. However, if I'm elected, you can be assured that Trial Town will become a much more fiscally responsible organization than it is today."

I was amazed at how Paul completed his answer almost exactly at one minute.

Peggy then faced Jim Peck. "Mr. Peck, can you comment on any changes that you'd make to Trial Town's current spending habits?"

Jim Peck straightened his green tie. "Peggy, I want to also thank you for providing this great venue to discuss Trial Town's future and the differences between my opponent and me. Unlike my opponent who cannot seem to name any programs he'd cut, I feel that Trial Town has not invested enough in our fine community. I believe that Trial Town can do a much better job at additional funding for schools, support for our elderly, and much improved park systems for our citizens to enjoy."

Like Paul, Jim Peck also completed his response at exactly one minute.

Peggy asked nine more questions and alternated between each candidate during the debate. I have to admit that I found some good responses to the questions by both candidates. However, I didn't feel the debate helped me decide on how I would ultimately vote.

Election Day came and went, and we ended up with the election of three Green Party candidates and three Red Party candidates. It seemed like our two-party system was an amazing success... there was no winner with less than a 55% voter approval rating in their individual race. I was looking forward to a great two-year session with my new city council, knowing that whatever opinions expressed would be those of the majority of citizens of Trial Town.

It had been a month since the excitement of the elections had ended and we all met at the City Hall for our first meeting. Our first city council meeting was interesting. The three newly elected Red Party members had big R's next to their names; the three Green Party members had big G's next to their names, indicating their party affiliations.

I welcomed all of the new members. "Okay… first of all, congratulations to all of the recent winners of our elections here in Trial Town. I believe that you've all demonstrated that our two-party system is an amazing success and I'm looking very much forward to having such well-supported members of my city council for the next two years."

I then decided to get down to business. "One of the most pressing issues facing our city is the construction of sidewalks along our Main Street. Many citizens have pointed out that all major towns have sidewalks on their main streets and we really ought to have them as well. The cost of this project has been estimated at approximately $1 million. We will need to raise these funds with new taxes in order to complete the project in the next two years. The cost to each person in Trial Town will be approximately $2 per year for the next seven years."

It was at this point that I got the strangest reaction. Paul Fredrick, one of the Red Party members, blasted, "You've got to be kidding, Mayor! I ran my political campaign on being financially responsible and reducing the cost of operating Trial Town…. And the first order of business you have for us is a $2 per year tax increase for every Trial Town citizen?"

As I opened my mouth to speak, Sally Hatfield piped up. "You Reds are not interested in anything that can make our town a better place. It's always about the dollars. Two dollars per year per person is nothing if it means not getting run over by cars that race through our main street."

Then an even stranger thing happened. All city council members felt it would be best if they consulted with their individual parties on the sidewalk issue before they offered any further opinions. I thought to myself, "This must be the way a two-party government works."

Back at Green Party headquarters, the three Green Party city council members discussed the situation with several others from the Green Party organization. It was settled; the three Green Party members not only wanted the sidewalks built, they felt the sidewalk issue had such great appeal to the voters, they would slip in a few Green Party promised projects into the sidewalk decision to get those passed as well. After all, they thought, "Mayor Wallaby would vote 'yes' on the sidewalk project as he was the one recommending it in the first place". They thought, "this would be a 4-3 vote that would rule the day, regardless of what those cheap Reds wanted". And in case any of the Green Party members were not aware… any vote in opposition to the party line would be met with no Green Party campaign funds for their next election.

Back at Red Party headquarters, the three Red Party city council members were discussing the situation along with several others from the Red Party organization. They all had mixed feelings. They did agree that their town needed sidewalks along Main Street. However, they were also committed to operating the Trial Town government at a lower cost than it had been operated previously. They were settled… the sidewalk project could only go ahead if the added tax burden could be eliminated by cutting other costs within Trial Town's city budget. And in case any of the Red Party members were not aware… any vote in opposition to the party line would be met with no Red Party campaign funds for their next election.

As we convened the next city council meeting, I opened with, "So I trust that all of you have had ample opportunity to discuss the Main Street Sidewalk issue with your respective parties. What questions or concerns do you have about moving forward with this worthy project?"

Sally spoke up immediately, "Mayor, we Green Party members were so pleased to see that you have recognized that our city really needs Main Street sidewalks and we are in full support of this project. However, we don't believe this sidewalk project goes far enough. The Green Party believes that we could use two large parks to improve the recreation opportunities in our city. It seems petty to ask voters for $2 per year per person for sidewalks when we could be asking for $10 per year per person and make a noticeable improvement to Trial Town."

Upon hearing this, I noticed the faces of my Red Party city council members turning red. Paul could hold his tongue no longer, "What kind of planet are you Greenies living on? We Red Party members have a much more responsible proposal. We'll support the construction of the sidewalks along Main Street but won't support a tax increase to pay for these improvements. We believe that there are costs that can be saved within the city's current $10 million per year budget that will allow us to fund this project within our current tax income. We further believe that we can find sufficient cost savings to give citizens of Trial Town a $10 per year per person tax reduction."

Only thirty minutes into our city council meeting, I could see we were at an impasse. The Red Party members would not yield on their position to cut taxes and the Green Party members would not yield on their position to complete several city projects. I then spoke up. "Well, ladies and gentlemen, I am also a voting member of this council and I do not like either of your proposals. First, I don't agree that we need two additional parks at this time and don't believe this added tax will be supported by our public. Second, I'm aware that you city council members are new to our council and don't know all of ins and outs of the city budget. But I highly doubt that we can find $1 million for the sidewalks let alone additional cuts that would enable a tax decrease."

Sally then chimed in. "Say, Mayor, what party do you want to belong to for your next election? Green or Red?"

My heart sank. I realized where this question was going. I would have to run for re-election next year and would need to affiliate with one party or the other. I suppose I could start a third party, but I was clearly aware of the amount of money that was already held by the Red and Green parties. I would go through a high-intensity election just like these city council members and either win or lose. If I sided with the Green Party in this decision and other decisions to come, I would be a sure winner for the Green Party in an upcoming campaign. Likewise, for the Red Party. Although both party platforms seemed respectable, the resulting actions of each party were so extreme. I simply could not join one of these groups.

I responded, "Sally, I'm still considering my options at this point. At present, I'm not very happy with how the two-party system is affecting our day-to-day decision making as a city council. If this is how things work, I can't see joining either party. " Trying to get the discussion back to Trial Town's sidewalks, I continued, "How about we talk through this decision? Is there any information regarding this decision that will change your position?"

Paul was the first to speak up. "I can't speak for any of the Greenies but as for all of us in the responsible Red Party, we'll need to see better numbers in order to make any budget recommendations. Under no circumstances will any of my Red Party colleagues support any tax increase."

Sally then reacted predictably. "I believe I do speak for our gracious Green Party when I say that we genuinely care about our community and have been elected by folks that also care about our community. We won't cave to these Reds and their greedy supporters who can't seem to afford a few pennies for desperately needed improvements to our town."

I responded, "It looks like we have a stalemate. I can't personally vote for either party's current proposal."

I adjourned the meeting, letting each member know that I needed to think about the situation further before I could make any further decisions on the city sidewalk issue.

When I picked up my copy of the Trial Town Gazette the following morning, I saw the proverbial icing on the cake. On the front page was printed the two statements by the city council members and some comment about me indicating that I could not demonstrate sufficient leadership qualities to pick a side. The article took up the entire front page. Then the phone calls started from members of both parties. I heard some of the most reprehensible language urging me to join their side or I was an idiot. In fact, if I didn't join their side, they would use their financial resources to embarrass me in any way they could. I could hear emotional tones in calls from both sides. These folks had fully bought into whatever they felt their parties represented.

Our first issue out of the gate and it was clear that this two-party system had some major flaws. In our past, we would have discussed the topic of sidewalks and put the decision to a vote with each person voting their conscience. Usually, council members would ask me for budget details and the accuracy of cost estimates and more detail on the nature of the project. My sense is that the sidewalk measure would have passed as I presented it with last year's <u>no-party</u> city council.

Before I threw in the towel on the two-party system, I wanted to confirm that this was not some anomaly so I called Don Westland, the mayor of Capital City.

"Say, Mayor," I started, "Trial Town has attempted the two-party system that you were telling me about in our lunch meeting. At first, I thought things were going great as we got through the election process. However, when I sat down with my newly elected city council for the first time, I was shocked that they couldn't come to a consensus on the easiest decisions. Is this how things have been working in Capital City?"

Don laughed. "Yes, yes, yes… you have those pesky ideologies leaking into each decision. You have it rough your first time out. You have an equal number of members from each party. That's a recipe for deadlock. Here in Capital City, we have always had a majority of one party or the other and we tend to make decisions fully biased toward the majority party. The minority party rarely gets their opinion heard."

I felt I needed to fill Don in on our situation. "I have to tell you, Mayor, both party's ideas in our most recent city council meeting were downright nutty. I couldn't have imagined picking either side's idea."

"Yes, we've done some whacky things that were promoted by the majority party in Capital City."

"How can you run a city government that way?"

"When the majority party makes whacky decisions, they pay in the next election and the opposing party gets a turn at the majority. Then we have whacky decisions that go to the other extreme."

I persevered with my question. "Mayor, how on earth can you run your city by going one direction and then the other?"

"After many cycles of changing majority parties, the party decisions seem less whacky. I have to say that I don't think we've ever done what I believed is the 'right thing' for our citizens as we have caved to the wackiness of the majority party."

"One more question. How did you decide which party to join yourself?"

He laughed. "That's a no-win proposition. In Capital City, the mayor is not allowed to belong to either party system so that's my free pass."

I closed our conversation. "Thanks, Mayor. You've been very helpful in guiding me to my final decision regarding our two-party system."

After my talk with Don, I thought more about what was actually happening. In our past system, I was concerned that elected officials may only represent a minority of the population. However, once these city council members were elected, they would need to accommodate the majority of the population or they would not be re-elected.

I addressed my city council in our next meeting. "I believe that it would be best to abolish the two-party election system for Trial Town for the following reasons:

1) Parties have created a polarizing effect in our city council and in our communities that appears to force all to pick a side regardless of any logical direction for our city.

2) In city council meetings, both parties have taken diametrically opposed positions. And, each party won't relinquish their position to hear opposing views to work toward a viable compromise.

3) If we were to have a majority of any one party in our council, we would most likely be subject to some very whacky and ideologically biased decisions that wouldn't serve our citizens well and would create inefficiency in our government, as each majority party would try to undo what the previous majority party had done.

4) If any party member breaks rank with their party for rational reasons, they are threatened with no financial support by their party in upcoming elections.

5) Biases that affect important political decisions confuse the decisions that need to be made and are intended to enlist political support that's counter to conducting the business of Trial Town in a reasonable way.

Sally Hatfield spoke first. "Mayor, I'm somewhat confused. Why did you believe Trial Town would benefit from a two-party system in the first place?"

"I felt a larger percentage support in a general election would imply that elected city council members would better represent our citizens. Instead, I've found that parties and not politicians hold the actual political power in a two-party system."

Paul Fredrick chimed in. "I'm not sure I understand the problem with party influences."

"All parties have some very admirable principles in their respective platforms. Unfortunately, these ideals become polarizing forces on our board and in our community."

Paul asked, "What do you mean by 'polarizing'?"

"Let's take our recent sidewalk issue. One party wants to reduce taxes by $10 per year per person while the other wants to increase taxes by $10 per year per person. We simply need to build sidewalks. Polarization is when two sides establish untenable positions based on 'supposed' ideals and won't compromise."

Paul continued, "Are you saying that controlling spending is a bad thing?"

"Paul, controlling spending is important but it isn't the only thing that should drive city council decisions."

Sally interrupted. "Are you saying that you don't want parks for our city's citizens?"

"Sally, we have two large parks that seem to serve our citizens well. In addition, I don't think that most citizens of Trial Town can afford a large tax increase."

Sandy, a Trial Town Gazette reporter attending the city council meeting, spoke up. "What will happen to the current city council members?"

I responded. "I propose that we keep every member in their current position as elected and simply eliminate party titles. My sense is that we'll have much more reasonable give-and-take discussions once parties have less say in the actions of individual members of this city council."

I had expected a major battle; however, it appeared that most members seemed to understand my logic. I did get a lot of push back by party leaders though.

The Green Party president, Hal Sparks, spoke up. "Mayor, this is a complete outrage. These city council members were voted into office by large funding contributions by us parties. If the city council abolishes parties, I believe you are telling all party members that you don't respect their decisions."

"Hal, I believe that these same city council members would have most likely been elected even in our previous election system. Further, my sense is that even party voters aren't happy with the stalemate that has resulted in our two-party system."

The Red Party president, Grace Frampton, asked, "Mayor, if you abolish the two-party system, what do you propose the parties do with all of the funds we have raised to support our candidates?"

I was caught a little off guard by this question. "Grace, I believe the parties ought to fund future candidates that best reflect your individual ideals."

Grace seemed less than pleased with my response.

After our discussion, we voted to repeal the two-party system law; the vote was unanimous 6-0. Grace Frampton and Hal Sparks were noticeably furious and continued to try to influence the city council members they elected. Eventually, both parties ran out of money as Trial Town citizens started to understand the same problems that our city council had discovered with the two-party system.

To try to establish more of a mandate for elected city council candidates, we established a two-tier election process. If a winning candidate got less than 45% of the total vote in the original election, we would hold an additional vote between the top two candidates. This would ensure that the winning candidate would receive a legitimate majority vote by all voters. Mayor Westland from Capital City thought that this was such a good idea that Capital City also abandoned their two-party system in favor of the two-tier voting process.

Real World Examples

The current US Congress, executive and judicial branches are highly polarized. The Republican Party and Democrat Party raise billions of dollars that can be utilized by their favorite candidates. We routinely have government shutdowns, budget impasses and gridlock whenever we get close to a balanced political system. When one party dominates the political scene, large, sweeping, highly partisan laws are passed as soon as these majority parties gain control.

One such legislation was the Affordable Care Act (Obama Care). The problem posed to all lawmakers was quite straightforward:

1) Health insurance costs for most Americans were out of control, increasing at double the cost of inflation on an annual basis, causing employers to drop coverage for most employees.

2) Most insurance companies that covered individuals under non-employer programs would not cover pre-existing conditions, eventually being virtually ineffective.

3) Low income earners could not afford health insurance in any form, as they simply did not have this added income if their employer would not pay up the cost.

The discussion of the healthcare topic became polarized very quickly, with Republicans indicating that they would not support any kind of national health care plan; and Democrats forcing through the resulting Affordable Care Act. There was limited conversation between Republicans and Democrats to arrive at a logical decision that considered both party's concerns. Democrats wanted to pass their law. Republicans wanted to stop the law with no alternative.

Now think about this for a minute. If our politicians had actually wrestled with the problems presented, understood the impact and how we could still solve most of the problems without creating a financially unsustainable system; wouldn't we all be better off?

So here we are with an unworkable solution.

Republican majorities make bad decisions as well. George W. Bush passed the Medicare Modernization Act in 2003 in the face of budget deficits that eventually grew to $10 trillion in government debt by the time he exited office in 2008.

The voting public is somewhat aware that it is dangerous to have a complete majority of one party in power for any length of time. Among the last three presidents, Barack Obama, George Bush and Bill Clinton; each has enjoyed had their own party in power for only 25% of their collective years in office.

Polarization results in the elimination of logic and good analytical decisions. If you are a Democrat or Republican, you must vote with your party or you are not considered a "team player." This polarization not only affects politicians, but also is common in folks voting for politicians. If you ask most people why they voted for one candidate over the other, they would cite some emotional party line that's quite ridiculous. When you question these folks a little further on specific issues and stances, they cannot rationalize their position. In fact, I believe this is why many people don't like to discuss politics. They believe what they believe and find it difficult to defend their position. It's like the old saying; "People buy on emotion and justify with logic". My hope is that people will start to better understand issues and hold their politicians accountable for how they vote.... And not just on election day.

2 Robin Hood Syndrome

"To take from one, because it is thought his own industry and that of his fathers has acquired too much, in order to spare to others, who, or whose fathers, have not exercised equal industry and skill, is to violate arbitrarily the first principle of association, the guarantee to everyone the free exercise of his industry and the fruits acquired by it."
— Thomas Jefferson

One thing I noticed as I walked the streets of Trial Town is that we have a very diverse population of folks. Some people have been very fortunate in their business dealings and have made substantial wealth for themselves, while others are struggling. At first, I thought the folks that were struggling were to blame for their circumstances. After all, everyone in Trial Town has plenty of opportunity to make it on their own. It was then that I started to learn a few of my poorer constituents' stories.

Emma Parkinson is a single mother. After getting pregnant in high school, she had her first baby boy. Emma did not marry the father of her son. She also never made it to one of our fine colleges in Trial Town. As it happened, she had two more children. Again, no father stuck around. She now works two minimum wage jobs barely supporting her three kids and herself.

Then there is Charlie Mackey. Charlie is single and does not have a family. He was recently laid off a job that he held for five years. He was not trained for anything else that would give him a similar income, nor did he feel he could work for a minimum wage job to make ends meet.

After learning about Charlie and Emma's individual situations, I had the chance to have dinner at the house of one of our more distinguished citizens, James Pennyworth. James had it all… he had the large house on a hill; three children enrolled in private schools and a beautiful wife. He made his fortune in the paper production business, having started his business early in his life and working hard. He was lucky enough to come up with some innovations in paper that allowed his business to prosper. I really respected James. He was smart, worked hard and had done quite well for himself.

I felt these individual people were not that different, except for the circumstances dealt them by life. It was therefore unfair that James would live in a state of "excess" with money in the bank and more coming in daily, while two other citizens of Trial Town suffered and had very few resources.

Trial Town had always followed a flat income tax plan with all citizens paying 15% of their income in taxes. There were no frills and people seemed to like it that way. But I felt this was putting too much of the financial burden on the poor folks who could least afford to pay these taxes.

I knew what I had to do. Somehow, I needed to get James to pay more taxes and reduce the tax burdens on Emma and Charlie to improve their lot in life. Here is my three-step plan to even things out. I call it the Even-Steven Plan:

1) We will tax any incomes above $100k/yr at 30%;

2) There will be no income tax at all for individual incomes less than $100k/yr; and

3) If you make less than $25k/yr, Trial Town will pay you $5k/yr to help make ends meet.

This was literally a stroke of brilliance. Since 70% of Trial Town's taxpayers made less than $100 thousand a year, they were all pleased with the plan. Prior to this plan, everyone was paying 15% of their income in taxes. I illustrated how both plans will allow Trial Town to collect their needed $1.4 billion in income tax revenue, while the Even-Steven Plan would create a much better situation for the less fortunate.

For folks in the lower tax brackets, their average after-tax income would increase from $12,500 per year to $20,000 per year. While the middle-income bracket payers would see their after- tax income rise from $59,500 to $70,000 per year. The wealthy in our community would see their income drop from $144,500 per year to $119,500 per year. I felt this was a small price to pay for the benefits bestowed on the majority of Trial Town's citizens.

Flat Tax Plan

Income Bracket	% Pop	# of Tax Payers	Average Income / person	Total Income ($000)	Tax Revenues ($000)	Individual After Tax Income
Under $25k/yr	10%	10,000	$ 15,000	$ 150,000	$ 22,500	$ 12,750
$25k/yr to $100k/	60%	60,000	$ 70,000	$ 4,200,000	$ 630,000	$ 59,500
Over $100k/yr	30%	30,000	$ 170,000	$ 5,100,000	$ 765,000	$ 144,500
Government Income					$ 1,417,500	

Even-Steven Plan

Income Bracket	% Pop	# of Tax Payers	Average Income / person	Total Income ($000)	Tax Revenues ($000)	Individual After Tax Income
Under $25k/yr	10%	10,000	$ 15,000	$ 150,000	$ (50,000)	$ 20,000
$25k/yr to $100k/	60%	60,000	$ 70,000	$ 4,200,000	$ -	$ 70,000
Over $100k/yr	30%	30,000	$ 170,000	$ 5,100,000	$ 1,530,000	$ 119,000
Government Income					$ 1,480,000	

When I announced the plan to my city council, I received great support by the majority of our council members. I believe that they knew that supporting the Even-Steven Plan would easily get them a majority vote when election season rolled around.

During the first year roll out of the plan, my tax collector, Sammy, came to me with concern on his face.

"What's wrong?" I asked Sammy in a jovial tone.

"Your new tax plan is what's wrong," grumbled Sammy.

I didn't get it… I knew that Sammy was one of those who would benefit as his personal tax payments were reduced from 15% to 0%. How in the world could he be disappointed with the new tax plan?

"Okay. What specifically is wrong with the Even-Steven tax plan?" I asked him.

"I have noticed that Trial Town's income from taxes for the year is down by half of what it was with our old plan."

I was now getting a little irritated. "Now, Sammy, you helped me run the numbers and we both agreed that the plan should give Trial Town the same tax revenue as before."

"Now just let me explain my findings before you interrupt."

"Okay. I'm listening."

Sammy proceeded. "When I did some digging, I discovered three things that are causing our decreased tax revenues… The first thing is that people who were making a little more than $25,000 per year felt they could make more money by dropping their income to below the $25,000 per year threshold."

I had to interrupt. "Are you kidding me, Sammy? I simply don't believe you."

"Remember Emma Parkinson? She quit her second job, reducing her $26,500 a year to $18,500 a year and is now making an after-tax income of $23,500 a year."

I felt a little proud of myself at this point. "Now, see Sammy? I knew that you were wrong. Emma isn't making more money than she made before. As a 'math' guy you probably know that $23,500 is less than $26,500 so Emma is not making more money."

Sammy then responded, "When you deduct 15% from Emma's previous income of $26,500, Emma was making a net income of $22,500. So, Mayor, this 'math man' (air quotes added for effect) knows that $22,500 is less than $23,500. Emma's income has increased even though she has quit one of her jobs."

I smiled. "Sammy, Sammy, Sammy… don't you feel happy for Emma? She now has time to spend with her kids without that second job. I for one feel great."

Sammy shrugged. "Okay, Mayor, please let me continue with my two other points."

"Okay, okay, go ahead with your rant."

Sammy, noticeably annoyed at my comment, continued. "Similar to Emma, people who make just a little more than $100,000 per year have found a way to reduce their taxable income below the $100,000 threshold."

I had to interrupt. "Wait a minute. Are you telling me that people are taking pay cuts to avoid paying taxes?"

Sammy responded. "That's exactly what I'm saying. Think about it…. If you make $101,000 per year, you have to pay roughly $30,000 per year in taxes, making your net income $71,000 per year. If you take a pay cut to get $99,000 per year, you get to keep all of your money without paying a dime in taxes." Sammy then got sarcastic. "Even as a "non-math man" you have to know that $99,000 is more than $71,000."

I got the point that Sammy was making… even though I was somewhat annoyed. I then nodded and added, "Okay, Sammy, what is your third point?"

"Mayor, this third item is the biggest problem. Some of the wealthy business owners in Trial Town have decided to move their businesses to Capital City in order to avoid the higher tax rates here."

I had to react to this one. "Those greedy SOB's! They have so much… why are they short-changing those that are less fortunate in our community?"

Sammy acted as if he didn't hear my emotional response. "Mayor, the bottom line is that all of these three reactions to the Even-Steven-Plan are negatively impacting Trial Town's bottom line."

I calmed down. "Okay, Sammy, show me the numbers."

Sammy then handed me a sheet of paper with a table that showed all of the tax brackets with populations and all kinds of other stuff. My eyes quickly focused on the Income Tax Revenue column. Trial Town would receive this amount from income taxes.

Even-Steven Plan Results

Income Bracket	% Pop	# of Tax Payers	Average Income / person	Total Income ($000)	Tax Revenues ($000)	Individual After Tax Income
Under $25k/yr	15%	15,000	$ 15,000	$ 225,000	$ (75,000)	$ 20,000
$25k/yr-$100k/yr	65%	65,000	$ 70,000	$ 4,550,000	$ -	$ 70,000
Over $100k/yr	15%	15,000	$ 200,000	$ 3,000,000	$ 900,000	$ 140,000
Government Income					$ 825,000	

Sammy then asked, "Mayor, do you know what this table is saying?"

I reacted with a somewhat grumpy tone, "I'm not an idiot, Sammy. It looks like we're receiving $825 million with the Even-Steven Plan while we were receiving $1.4 billion with our flat-tax system. Surely there's some good news out of all of this, isn't there? Like the news that Emma was able to quit her second job and spend time with her kids. Now, that's a campaign story ready for print."

"There's some good news, Mayor. Most lower and mid-income bracket people spent their added income on goods and services within Trial Town's community. "

I was happy. "Now, there you go, Sammy. Why are you so negative? I'll bet this added spending increased tax revenues for Trial Town."

"These added expenditures did increase the income of many of our wealthy entrepreneurs in Trial Town. This showed up as an increase in average income of the highest tax bracket from $170,000 per year up to $200,000 per year."

"Let me get this straight. In the Even-Steven-Plan, the poor and average income earners are earning slightly less on average to avoid higher tax brackets. Yet there are fewer high-income earners. But the higher income earners that are still out there are earning even more money?"

"That's right. So now let me give you some bad news about the Even-Steven Plan."

"Sammy, I thought you just shared all the bad news. You mean there's even more?"

"Mayor, there are several items that I feel you should know about the Even-Steven-Plan that we didn't count on in our original analysis."

"Okay, Sammy, let's have it."

"Once business owners understood they had to pay higher taxes, they needed to collect higher profits in order to have the same reinvestment capital to put back into their companies."

"Sammy, these higher profits should have resulted in increased income for Trial Tow, not a lower tax income."

Sammy quickly responded, "You're right, Mayor. This increased revenue is reflected in the table that I just showed you."

"Okay, so what's the bad news?"

"These higher prices from the need for higher profits were paid by all consumers within Trial Town, including the low income and mid-income earners."

I was getting angry again. "So are you telling me that those greedy business owners forced less fortunate folks in our community to pay their increased income taxes?"

Sammy now seemed a little upset. "Mayor, as I just told you, these business owners need a certain amount of money to reinvest in their companies in order to continue to be in business. If they don't maintain these profit levels, they'll go out of business. Based on my calculations, it seems the increased costs of goods and services have almost wiped out the income tax advantage that was felt by the two lower income groups."

"Okay, Sammy, I think I understand. It's odd how our attempt to distribute a little more wealth to the lower income earners has resulted in no wealth distribution at all. If everyone is basically paying the same amount of money either in increased profits or increased taxes, why is Trial Town experiencing such a drop in tax income?"

"Mayor, as I have already pointed out, many income earners reduced their income from our original projections. That means we have less income. This alone reduced Trial Town's income by 30%."

"Okay, maybe we can tweak the tax brackets to prevent people from shifting their income down."

"Mayor, it isn't just the down shift in personal incomes."

"What else?"

"Many of the business owners who have stayed in Trial Town feel they may eventually need to leave our community in order to compete."

"Sammy, all companies in Trial Town have to pay the higher taxes. I don't believe they can't compete."

"Mayor, Trial Town companies have to compete with companies from Capital City and other locations. If these other companies don't have to pay higher taxes, they will be able to offer the same goods and services to our citizens at lower prices."

I recapped what I was hearing. "So let me get this straight. We have'nt redistributed any wealth because wealthy folks are just passing their tax increase on to lower income earners; lower income earners are opting to make even less money to avoid paying higher taxes; and companies may be leaving Trial Town in order to compete driving our tax income even lower?"

Sammy responded with some nervousness. "Mayor, that's not the end of it."

"You mean there's even more bad news about the Even-Steven-Plan?"

"The earnings gap between the wealthy and the not-so-wealthy has expanded, creating a perception by many lower income earners that the Even-Steven Plan needs to go even further in taxing the wealthy."

"You mean after trying to distribute wealth to lower income earners, they are now thinking that they need even more?"

Sammy nodded. "You got it. All of these problems are certainly bad in and of themselves but you and I have to figure out how we can operate our Trial Town government with only half our traditional income."

"Wow," I responded. "How could this great plan have gone so wrong? Maybe my tax moves were too severe. If I had made a gradually progressive tax plan, things would have worked better. Or maybe I should increase taxes even more on the wealthy, as many are saying?"

Sammy offered, "Mayor, haven't you learned anything from our conversation? Even if we double taxes on the wealthy again, that wouldn't get us the added income we need to keep our government running. That's assuming that we don't dig our income problem hole even deeper."

"Of course, Sammy you're right," I conceded.

I now had to figure out how I could go through all of the information that Sammy shared with me in front of our city council. I had to run through our conversation several times to fully understand how the Even-Steven-Plan had backfired so badly.

It was a brutal city council meeting. The meeting lasted for four hours and the only topic of discussion was repealing the Even-Steven-Plan. Even with all the facts, the city council voted 3-3 on repealing the plan. I had to vote in favor to break the tie.

The reaction from many in the public was terrible. No matter how I tried to explain, many folks still thought that we were favoring the wealthy by repealing the Even-Steven-Plan. Little did they know that it was necessary to keep Trial Town running. Folks started to appreciate our actions a little more when jobs started coming back to Trial Town as companies moved back.

I also learned a valuable lesson. In a thriving community, it's normal to have a gap in earning results with our citizens. Any attempt to close this gap can have disastrous results that are difficult to anticipate.

Real World Examples

Wealth redistribution has been attempted throughout mankind's history. Some wealth redistribution methods have taken the form of military conquest in taking wealth from monarchies; others have taken the form of communism or socialism where government takes assets from the wealthy and try to redistribute them. The most recent examples in the United States include a progressive tax system very similar to the one outlined the in the Trial Town story. However, because of the US tax code, wealthy people have several tax exemptions that means they do not pay a large portion of taxes, which exacerbates the problem. Over the years, the US has gravitated to a "double" wealth redistribution approach. In addition to the progressive taxing principles in this Trial Town story, the US government states that they will take the added taxes being collected from the wealthy and develop assistance programs for the poor. Such programs include unemployment benefits, welfare, food stamps, Medicaid, and some Social Security benefits. Unfortunately, all of the efforts to redistribute wealth in the US have resulted in the largest gap between the haves and have-nots we have ever seen.

The reality is that the wealthy need to reinvest their wealth or they will lose it. These investments are good for all. When we tax or penalize success, we create this odd counter culture where many income earners are simply not motivated to work harder for less money. Eventually, the productivity and financial success of our country can be ruined simply by politicians leveraging feelings of envy and disdain for the wealthy.

The irony is that all attempts at wealth redistribution push the real burden to the middle-class. Middle-class people are not poor enough to get any of the government handouts and they are not wealthy enough to get many of the tax breaks. Most politicians claim that their wealth redistribution efforts are to help the ailing middle-class… yet most programs they promote make it more difficult for the middle-class to become wealthy.

3 Spend Ourselves to Prosperity

"What did the taxpayers get out of the Obama stimulus? More debt. That money wasn't just spent and wasted - it was borrowed, spent, and wasted."
— Congressman Paul Ryan

I was shopping for groceries at our local grocery store when I ran into Ben Wellington. Ben is the owner of a local bank located here in Trial Town.

"How are things going at the bank?", I asked him.

Ben was noticeably distracted. "Not so good, Arthur. We had to foreclose on three loans this week. It seems like this has been a trend for the past few months."

"What gives?", I asked.

"It just seems to be a bad economy," Ben responded. "Many of these home owners have lost either one or two major sources of income, resulting in slow and then no payments on their mortgages. If this trend continues, our bank may be in financial trouble."

I really did not know what to say. "Sorry to hear about your problems, Ben. I hope things pick up in the near future."

"As do I," he remarked.

As I continued shopping at our grocery store, I ran into James Pennyworth, the owner of our local paper mill.

"How are things going at the mill?", I asked.

"So, so, Arthur," responded James. "Paper sales seem to be flat and may be decreasing so we may be laying workers off later this year."

"I'm sorry to hear that, James. Hopefully, things pick up in your business soon.", I offered.

"Me too, Arthur... layoffs aren't pleasant."

I went back to my office and set up a meeting with Sammy Penbrook, our tax collector. I wanted to see some broader statistics on Trial Town's economic situation. When I entered our conference room, I could tell that Sammy had prepared all of the information that I had requested prior to our meeting. He had several accounting ledger books, his laptop was open and there was a spreadsheet projected on our conference room projector screen.

"How's it going, Sammy?" I inquired as I entered the conference room.

Sammy responded, "I'm doing great, but I have a feeling you're not going to like some of the answers to the questions you gave me earlier in the day."

"Sammy, I can't really change any of the facts but I certainly want to know what's going on. Let's start with my first question. How do our unemployment numbers look for Trial Town?"

"It appears that unemployment has increased from 5% three years ago to 7% in the current year."

"You're right. That sounds terrible!" I responded. "Now for the second question: How are tax revenues for the past twelve months?"

"Our tax income seems to be way down. Our total annual tax revenue three years ago was $1.4 billion per year. However, tax revenue for the last twelve months was only $1.16 billion."

"How could our revenues be down that much and it not be noted in our city council meetings?"

Sammy said, "Actually, Mayor, I've been warning you and council members of these problems for the past several meetings. We currently spend approximately $1.4 billion on government services, but our income has dropped a whopping $300 million per year. This has resulted in a budget deficit of $300 million. Three years ago, we had a bank balance of $100 million so we just spent this, thinking that the economy would turn around and the bank balance would start going back up when tax revenues returned to normal. In the past three years, we have gone from having $100 million in the bank to now having a debt of $288 million."

"Well, it doesn't look like it's returning to normal. It looks like the debt situation will get much worse next year if we don't do something."

Sammy folded his arms with a look of disgust on his face. "You've got it… I've been saying this for the past several months."

"No need to get defensive, Sammy. I'm sorry I didn't listen in the past. I really need to think about this situation before our next city council meeting. Your information has been very helpful."

"Any time."

The situation seemed depressing. Trial Town's tax revenues were dropping while, it seemed, several folks in our community were experiencing some real financial pain. I had heard that governments could stimulate the economy by injecting funds into it and get things jump-started. Maybe that is what we should do in this situation. I could not just sit idle while our citizens were in this situation. I thought a long time about it and felt I had a good plan to turn Trial Town's economy around.

It was a nice fall day for our next city council meeting. The leaves were turning and the temperature outside was not too hot or too cold. The topic of our meeting, on the other hand, was going to be quite heated. I really felt there was something we could do as a city government to turn our economic situation around and had developed a plan to stimulate Trial Town's economy with various projects that would both benefit our community and provide the needed jump-start our economy needed.

As I entered our city council room, I was glad to see all members were present as we all needed to weigh in on the topics that I wanted to cover. After the traditional preamble to our city council meeting, I opened up new business with a presentation by Sammy Penbrook. Sammy gave our council members the same information that he had given me only a few days earlier.

After Sammy was done, I showed an excerpt of Sammy's table that he had presented earlier in our meeting.

Predicted Status Quo

Year	Tax Revenues ($000)	Government Expenses ($000)	Interest + Income/ - Cost ($000)	Net + Surplus / - Deficit ($000)	Cash + Reserve / - Debt ($000)
-3	$ 1,400,000	$ (1,400,000)		$ -	$ 100,000
-2	$ 1,250,000	$ (1,400,000)	$ 3,000	$ (147,000)	$ (47,000)
-1	$ 1,160,000	$ (1,400,000)	$ (1,410)	$ (241,410)	$ (288,410)
0	$ 1,044,000	$ (1,400,000)	$ (8,652)	$ (364,652)	$ (653,062)
1	$ 939,600	$ (1,400,000)	$ (19,592)	$ (479,992)	$ (1,133,054)
2	$ 845,640	$ (1,400,000)	$ (33,992)	$ (588,352)	$ (1,721,406)
3	$ 761,076	$ (1,400,000)	$ (51,642)	$ (690,566)	$ (2,411,972)
4	$ 700,000	$ (1,400,000)	$ (72,359)	$ (772,359)	$ (3,184,331)
5	$ 700,000	$ (1,400,000)	$ (95,530)	$ (795,530)	$ (3,979,861)
6	$ 700,000	$ (1,400,000)	$ (119,396)	$ (819,396)	$ (4,799,257)
7	$ 700,000	$ (1,400,000)	$ (143,978)	$ (843,978)	$ (5,643,235)
8	$ 700,000	$ (1,400,000)	$ (169,297)	$ (869,297)	$ (6,512,532)
9	$ 700,000	$ (1,400,000)	$ (195,376)	$ (895,376)	$ (7,407,908)
10	$ 700,000	$ (1,400,000)	$ (222,237)	$ (922,237)	$ (8,330,145)

"Okay, so you see the financial situation we seem to find ourselves in. If our economy continues to trend the way it has been over the past three years, our future looks ugly. We had a cash reserve of $100 million three years ago, and we'll end our current year with total debt of roughly $288 million. As you can see by Sammy's projections, we may be in dire financial straits at the end of ten years."

Before I had a chance to finish, Paul Fredrick spoke up. "Mayor, what would happen if we simply reduce our government costs? It seems like all of this worry would go away if we just spend within our means."

Knowing that Paul would certainly be the type to cut costs at any sign of a budget deficit, I quickly responded, "Paul, if we reduce costs, I believe that this economy will get worse. After all, if we lay people off, our revenues will decline further. I've put together a stimulus plan to get our economy back on track so that we won't need to concern ourselves with reducing Trial Town City costs." I then showed my plan up on the overhead projector.

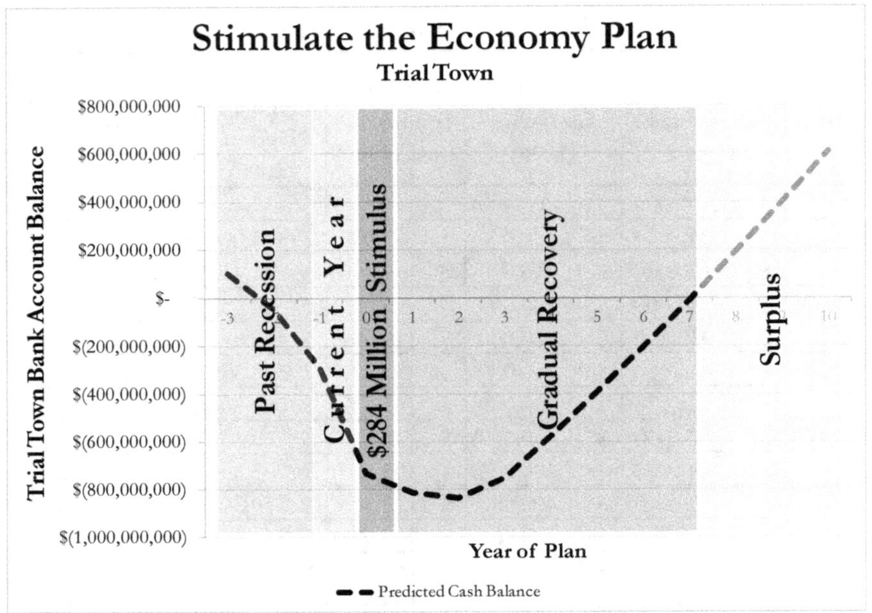

"I have estimated that if we invest $284 million in economic stimulus projects, Trial Town will be back to where we were before and even better. In my plan we would spend $70 million on energy efficiency projects; $107 million on road maintenance projects; and another $107 million on a new city park."

Sally Hatfield squinted her eyes in confusion. "I don't get it, Mayor. How can we pay an additional $284 million into our budget when we will already have a negative balance in our bank account?"

"Sally, we will have to borrow the money. I believe we'll be able to convince any banker that this is a sound plan that will allow us to pay back this debt over the next eight years."

Stan Smith was sitting next to Paul Fredrick and put in his two cents' worth. "Mayor, what happens if the revenue that you have predicted doesn't materialize as a result of this stimulus plan?"

I said, "I have no crystal ball about what will happen if we don't make this investment in the stimulus plan. But I do know what will happen if we do nothing at all. It seems we need to do something."

The discussion went on through the night until it finally ended in a vote at 1 a.m. I voted yes along with three city council members. Although this measure passed, it was clearly not popular with our entire city council.

After catching up on my sleep, I was ready to visit the bank along with Sammy Penbrook. Sammy and I walked into the bank together. I told the bank clerk welcoming us at the front of the bank that we wanted to talk to

Ben Wellington. We were then walked back through a modest bank lobby into Ben's nice corner office.

"Hi Ben," I said.

"What brings you two to the bank?" Ben queried.

"We would like to give you some business." I then proceeded to explain the stimulus plan that we were anticipating for Trial Town and how it would help the economy.

Ben reacted positively. "That's great news! I can't see the city defaulting on a loan. I really need good loans to get this bank back on its feet and I really want Trial Town's economy to come back so I can stop attending bank loan foreclosure meetings."

I said, "I would like a line of credit of $1 billion for our plan to work fully. We need funds for our stimulus project investments and we will need to borrow money in future years for predicted budget deficits."

Ben said, "Arthur, $1 billion is a lot of money for our small bank. However, we can probably come up with half of it. I can also get a Capital City bank to pick up the other half. Trial Town has been run well in the past so I don't think getting the funds will be a problem."

"Sammy," I said, "lunch is on me… It's time to celebrate our new stimulus program. I believe this will save our town."

After a great lunch with Sammy, I got back to my office to find a few newspaper and TV reporters wanting to get all of the details. I proudly rolled out the plan the same way that I had in the city council meeting yesterday. The reporters seemed to like the program and I felt they would all give it great press.

It was about 4:00 p.m. and I was going to call it a day. We got great news from the bank, a long lunch with Sammy and a great press conference with our town's finest reporters. I deserved to take off early.

It had been a week since we started planning many of the stimulus plan projects. Besides a few whiny city council members, I really had heard nothing negative about our stimulus program. I heard my secretary's voice over the office intercom. "James Pennyworth says that he'd like to meet with you. What should I tell him?"

"Please send him in," I said.

As James entered my office, I bragged, "Did you hear about our new economic stimulus plan?"

"Arthur, that's what I'd like to talk to you about," James said.

Here it comes. Now I am going to be congratulated by one of the best financial minds in our community. I was beaming with pride with the positive articles written in our local newspaper. "James did you see that full spread in the Trial Town Gazette?"

"I did, Arthur," James responded. "At first blush, I have to tell you, I'm not happy with this plan."

James must have noticed the shock on my face. "I don't understand, James. I think that this stimulus will be great for your business. You said yourself you were concerned about your paper mill and the trend of our current economy. If this plan works, your business should pick up. I don't get your skepticism."

"I understand that our economy is down, but we've gone through these times before and will be able to weather this one no differently," said James. "The problem with this stimulus plan is that it's showing that Trial Town's government cannot reduce its costs as the economy pulls back a little. To make matters worse, you borrow more money to attempt to stimulate Trial Town's economy. To me this action is forcing citizens to pay a much higher bill sometime in the future. All of us business owners expect that we will end up paying this tax bill at some point. This gives me even more stress about my company's future here in Trial Town."

I stopped James. "Please, James, listen to reason."

James went on, "Look, I'm not sure what these Trial Town funds will do for the playground, road building or energy efficiency industries, but these projects don't directly benefit my company. In addition, the only thing that I know is that I'm going to have a higher tax bill in the future to pay for this mistake."

I felt James was just getting cranky about nothing. Just like my whiny city council members. I was confident that our plan would succeed. "James, I'll make you a wager. If this program works, you owe me a steak dinner. If it fails, as you seem to think, then I owe you a steak dinner. Deal?"

James smiled. "You've got yourself a bet! I can taste that steak now."

Over the next few months, we were busy identifying and defining projects ready to complete with stimulus funds. The parks and road projects were handled by the city. The way we implemented the energy efficiency projects was through a rebate program. Trial Town would pay 50% of the cost of any project that would reduce energy consumption for any building owned by a Trial Town citizen.

We did have to reassign several city staff to handle the stimulus projects but we had plenty of extra staff since it seemed that our normal work was somewhat slow.

In order to stimulate the economy, we made a self-imposed condition to spend all of the funds in this first year of the program. That way we would jump-start the economy and we could see the immediate positive impact of the stimulus program.

After a lot of hard work by city officials and many contractors, we did it. We spent all of our stimulus funds in a single year. I was anxious to get back in front of the city council with Sammy to review our results for our first year of the stimulus. I think I was even more anxious to get the steak dinner promised by James Pennyworth.

I set up my pre-meeting with Sammy to see how things were going. Again, as I walked into the conference room, Sammy was all prepared. I did not waste any time with small talk. "Sammy, how did we do?"

"Well," said Sammy, "The unemployment numbers do not look a lot different from last year. In fact, full-time unemployment has increased from 7% last year to 8% this year."

"What?" I exploded. "We just implemented three major projects. That had to improve our unemployment situation!"

"You'd think so," said Sammy, "According to my numbers, employment did increase in some of the directly impacted fields like road construction, grounds construction and some of the energy efficiency trades; however, in almost all other industries, unemployment rates increased."

"Do you have any idea why unemployment would be high in other companies?"

"I did have a chance to talk to several business owners in Trial Town. They claim that they didn't like the stimulus program because it would result in a higher tax bill down the road. They told me they were reluctant to hire new employees, not knowing what their final tax liability would be in the future with such aggressive spending by the government."

I had become noticeably upset. "That's great! Here we are trying to stimulate the economy and a few Nervous Nellies' pull back on employment because they don't believe in my plan. Enough about unemployment. What about tax revenues? Did those increase as predicted?"

"It's not too bad on revenues. You had anticipated tax revenues to increase from $1,160,000 to $1,250,000. However, revenues stayed flat at $1,160,000," Sammy stated.

"Are you kidding me? We pump $284 million into our economy and have flat-tax revenues? That must mean that Trial Town's economic situation may have been worse than we had originally anticipated. Had we done nothing, our tax revenue income would be way down!"

I then presented these same results to our city council. Again, Paul Fredrick implored me to consider cost reductions on the city budget to help reduce our increasing debt.

I confidently told the council that we had stopped our tax revenue decline and should be back on track this coming year.

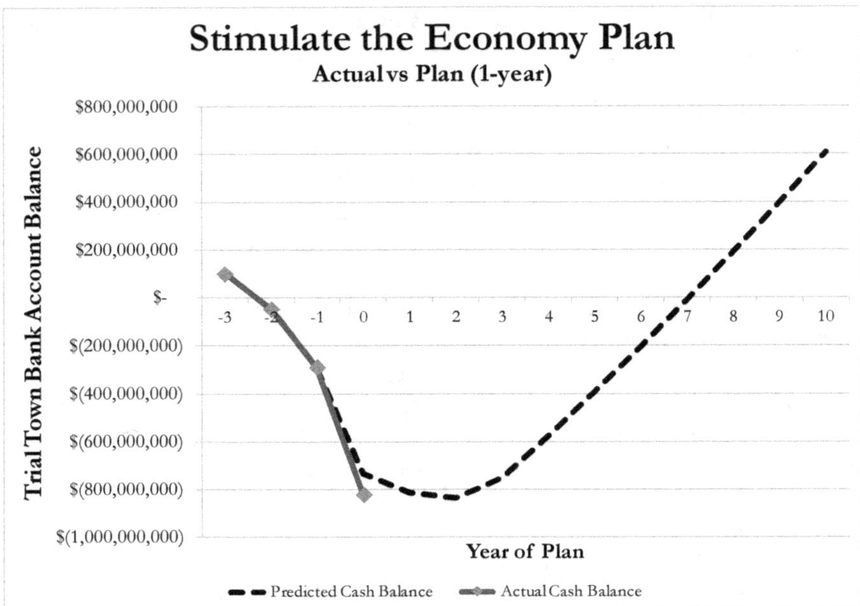

I humbly showed the city council the comparison of our expectations versus the actual results for this first year of our stimulus program. It was not going to be easy. Even if the plan had met expectations, we would still be $730 million in debt. It was not much worse to see $820 million in debt with our actual results.

This event took place each year for five years. Each year, I had to keep going back to the bank and asking that they increase our credit limit because we just kept getting further in debt as our budget deficit was never met by any added income. Each year I had to humbly sit in front of a restless city council explaining why our plan was not meeting its original expectations.

Here is what the chart looked like in year five.

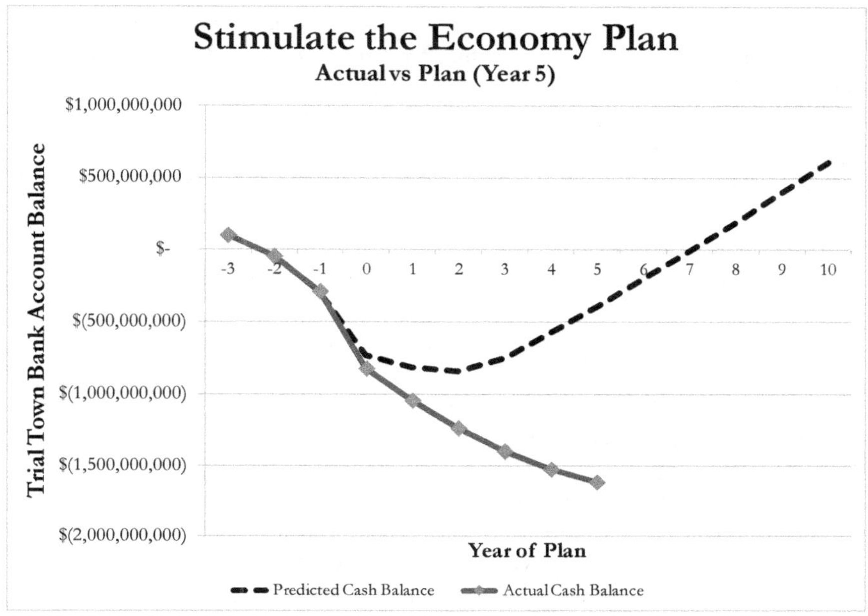

Instead of having a debt of $400 million at the end of our fifth year that would be shrinking with increased tax revenues, we had an outstanding debt of $1.6 billion; and our debt was growing each year. Our tax revenues had increased slowly over the last five years but not nearly enough to pay off our massive debt.

As I was sitting in my office almost in tears, I heard a knock on the door. "Come in," I said. My heart sank when I saw James Pennyworth stick his head through the door. I managed to speak. "I get it… you want to kick a guy while he's down."

James smiled. "Oh no. I came to collect on our bet. Will this Friday night work for you?"

"Okay, okay, you're right, you won our bet. I'll meet you at the Golden Steer at 6:00 p.m. this coming Friday," I replied. "Just one thing, James?"

"Sure," said James. "What do you need?"

"At our dinner I need you to tell me in more detail exactly why you knew our stimulus plan would fail?"

"Sure thing," said James. "I'll even bring you a few ideas on what would have worked better."

I met James in front of the Golden Steer just as we had discussed, and we were seated at our table. I noticed he was carrying a pad of paper. "So I see that you brought some paperwork with you. Are these papers going to show me where we went wrong?"

"I hope so, Arthur," said James.

Both James and I were seated. The waitress took our drink order. Both of us ordered iced tea to drink. I didn't want to drink anything stronger, as I felt I wanted to be completely sober for our discussion.

James jumped right in. "Arthur, I know that you're well-meaning with your stimulus program. But the reality is that government cannot act a whole lot different than any of us business owners when we're experiencing bad economic times."

"I don't understand."

"What do you think a business does when its revenues drop due to poor sales?" James asked.

"Well, I'm guessing that the business has to reduce its costs until sales recover," I said.

"Exactly," said James. "So why do you feel government should react differently? When Trial Town was experiencing financial problems, you recommended more spending. All this tactic gave us was more debt."

"Apparently, based on our latest accounts, Trial Town's debt is higher than it's ever been. But why didn't the funds that we put into our economy with our stimulus projects have any impact?" I asked.

"Trial Town did get a small blip, but nothing close to what you had hoped. If you invest an additional $284 million into our local economy, approximately 15% of that will make it back to Trial Town as tax revenue of $42.6 million. This was probably just enough not to show the negative impact of company owners like me who didn't like the stimulus program and so reduced investment in new employees over concerns of higher government debt being imposed."

"So you're saying our tax revenues in the first year were positively impacted by our stimulus projects. But these meager benefits were offset by skepticism of business owners who did not benefit from these stimulus projects?" I asked.

"Yes, that's exactly what I'm saying," said James.

"If that's the case, why did tax revenues gradually improve after the first year? It seems like the stimulus program stopped our bad economy from getting worse and then it created a slow growth in tax revenues. Granted, the growth wasn't as fast as I had hoped but it was certainly better than continuing our downward slide."

"Honestly, Arthur, like I said in your office five years ago, we go through good and bad times without government stimulus programs. The slow growth that you saw was a natural growth that would have happened without the stimulus."

"Okay, before our waitress takes our food order, tell me what you would have done differently."

"I'm glad you asked," James responded. He then reached into his pad of paper and pulled out a table that was similar to mine but had much different numbers.

Right-Size Government Plan

Year	Tax Revenues ($000)	Government Expenses ($000)	Stimulous Investment	Interest + Income/ - Cost ($000)	Net + Surplus / - Deficit ($000)	Cash + Reserve / - Debt ($000)
-3	$ 1,400,000	$ (1,400,000)			$ -	$ 100,000
-2	$ 1,250,000	$ (1,350,000)		$ 3,000	$ (97,000)	$ 3,000
-1	$ 1,160,000	$ (1,230,000)		$ 90	$ (69,910)	$ (66,910)
0	$ 1,160,000	$ (1,100,000)	$ -	$ (2,007)	$ 57,993	$ (8,917)
1	$ 1,218,000	$ (1,177,000)		$ (268)	$ 40,732	$ 31,815
2	$ 1,278,900	$ (1,259,390)		$ 954	$ 20,464	$ 52,280
3	$ 1,342,845	$ (1,347,547)		$ 1,568	$ (3,134)	$ 49,146
4	$ 1,400,000	$ (1,400,000)		$ 1,474	$ 1,474	$ 50,620
5	$ 1,400,000	$ (1,400,000)		$ 1,519	$ 1,519	$ 52,139

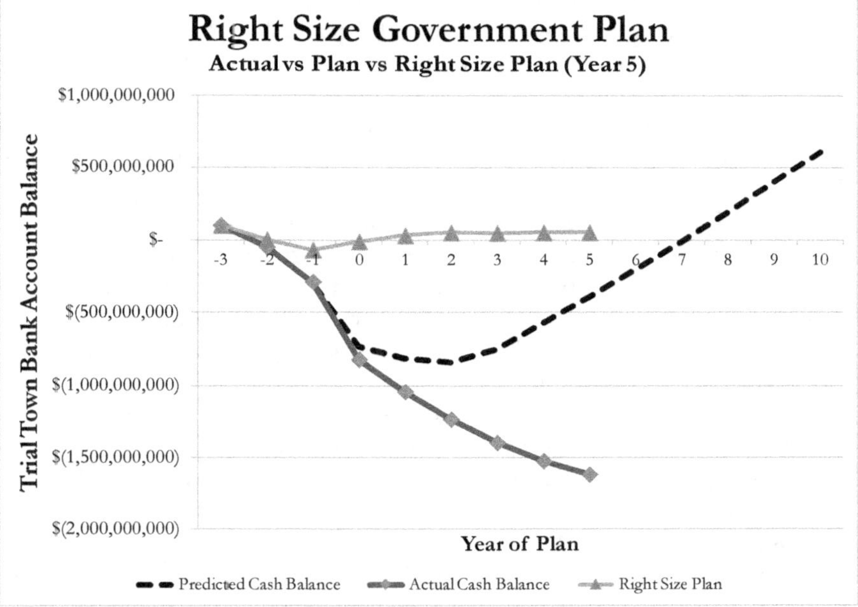

James started his explanation. "I want to go back three years, before Trial Town even thought about addressing the economic problem. If I were mayor, I would have started cutting costs when it was apparent that tax revenues were decreasing."

I interrupted, "Paul Fredrick wanted to do this, but I was convinced that we'd have simply been adding more folks to the unemployment rolls, making the economic situation even worse."

"You government people." James laughed. "By reducing your costs, similar to us businesses, Trial Town would have gained confidence from its business community that we wouldn't have a high future tax liability. This would have given us much more confidence to hire new employees when we needed them, knowing that there would not be some higher tax slapped on us down the road."

"Based on your model, you don't think that laid-off city employees would have negatively impacted our Town's tax revenues at all?" I asked in disbelief.

"That's right," responded James with confidence. "Whenever I lay off an employee, I feel bad because I feel I have cut off this person's ability to feed his or her family and make a livelihood. I then realized that when I lay off employees, they go through a time of turmoil and then they find other employment, or I would hire them back when things got better. When you treat employees like helpless victims of their employer, you're selling these valuable folks short. The reality is that if you don't need these employees, whether in the government or in a business, another business or government can use these workers. If you hold on to them, you're preventing them from reaching their full career potential and you're creating a financial drag on your government or business."

"I get it," I said. "Wow, I really had this all backwards." I then had to ask a question that had been on my mind for quite some time over the past five years. "James, why were so many other people so positive and supportive for this stimulus program if it had so many obvious flaws?"

James laughed. "Something that you'll need to know as mayor of Trial Town is that most people don't understand complex economic financial decisions. They see the short-term promised benefit and don't question the logic of anything else. Ben, the banker, was going to give a $1-billion loan to a client who was guaranteed to repay. How could he be sad about that? Other companies thought they would get a piece of some of the government money, so they were positive as well. Everyone else in the community thought that you were saving their jobs, and unemployment would get better.

"One additional point; Not everyone was positive about the stimulus program. You had three city council members who voted against the stimulus program. Their no vote may have been for some of the same reasons I have outlined in our discussion tonight. I'm guessing that these city council members were either ignored or couldn't articulate their concerns to convince you not to implement the stimulus program."

I asked, "What about the companies that did benefit from the stimulus projects? Didn't they go on to create jobs that wouldn't have been present otherwise?"

"Many of these companies did benefit for a very short time. The road construction company was able to avoid layoffs that they would have otherwise implemented. However, when this money was spent, these companies went ahead with their planned layoffs anyway. The money was only invested for a single year and went away."

I was utterly mortified. I had been so proud and felt such a genius when the bankers and the newspapers were singing my praises. I now felt so stupid after James showed me the errors of our planned stimulus program.

I humbly stated to James, "Trial Town has a debt of $1.6 billion because of my stimulus plan instead of a bank balance of $52 million with your spending cut plan. The even sadder thing is that the stimulus plan had no positive impact on our economy whatsoever. James, I think I'm going to consult you if I ever want to try something like this again."

"That's good to hear," James said. "Enough about business, let's order our dinner."

After our great meal, I used the magic of Trial Town's reset button, erased our large debt and started back where we had been before our stimulus program. I then implemented James' Right Size Government plan instead. Just as James had predicted, our economy did come back slowly on its own. In addition, we didn't have the massive debt that resulted from the stimulus program.

If we did not have the Trial Town reset button that allows us to erase and reset time, we would have had to pay that massive debt back. Our city council would have had to increase taxes just as James and other business owners had feared. My guess is that with this increased tax burden, our economic growth would have been much slower than the natural growth in our economy without the stimulus.

I learned a valuable lesson. Governments cannot stimulate an economy by more government spending.

Real World Examples

Throughout history, several politicians have attempted government stimulus programs. The reality is that almost all recessions and depressions have natural financial conditions that exist in our free market, or even social markets, that cannot be avoided. The two most popular stimulus programs in US history include Roosevelt's New Deal in the Great Depression and the more recent American Recovery & Reinvestment Act (ARRA), passed in 2009. Both programs have been proven to do almost nothing to the underlying economy. In both cases, growth was anemic compared to what it could have been with no stimulus program.

Prior to ARRA passed in 2009, George W. Bush doled out millions of taxpayer dollars to bail out banks and, most notably, General Motors, claiming that the US could not survive the housing bubble bursting in late 2008. Then ARRA was passed, adding an additional $800 billion of unadvertised bailouts plus an additional $2 trillion of guaranteed low/no interest loans to failing banks. The most recent ARRA program recovery was worsened when a tax increase was passed in 2011 in order to try to help pay the massive debt that was building, very similar to Trial Town's debt in year five of their stimulus program. An added burden to the US economic recovery is the high-cost health care bill called the Affordable Care Act (Obama Care) that was passed along with the stimulus program in 2009. Fortunately, the negative impacts of the ACA will not be felt until after 2015 when all provisions of this bill are in place. Many of the companies that received stimulus funds in 2009 went bankrupt shortly after the stimulus was spent, or have downsized to adapt to match economic conditions. The companies that have managed to generate the US economy during the stimulus program were not impacted by government funds through ARRA. In fact, the most profitable companies during the long and slow recovery were oil and gas production companies.

This was proof that the $800 billion ARRA stimulus program made almost no difference at all, except the additional debt that will now have to be repaid at some point. The national debt grew from $9.5 Trillion in 2008 to almost $18.5 Trillion in 2015. The administration is bragging that their annual budget deficits are dropping in this same time period. Much like Mayor Wallaby in the Trial Town stimulus program. Our nation's deficits would have been erased much quicker, if the government had controlled its spending to match our economic woes. Just like the Trial Town experience.

4 Government is the Answer

"A government big enough to give you everything you want, is a government big enough to take away everything that you have."
— Thomas Jefferson

Before we start this story, I feel it is important to fill the reader in on some basic facts about Trial Town. In our town, we are fully responsible for all government services. We get no funding assistance from federal, state or other organizations. This is part of the requirement of being a test government for others to model. A basic chart of the demographics of our citizens is shown below:

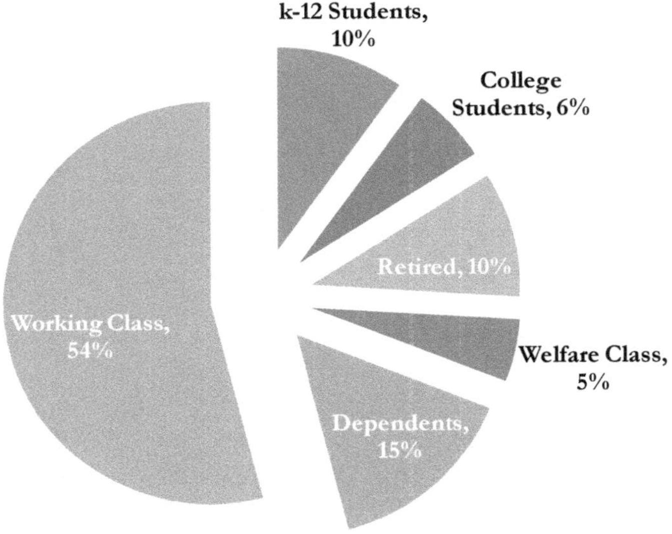

We have always had a fiscally responsible budgeting process in Trial Town that has resulted in an annually balanced budget. Our most recent budget of revenues and expenses are shown in the charts below:

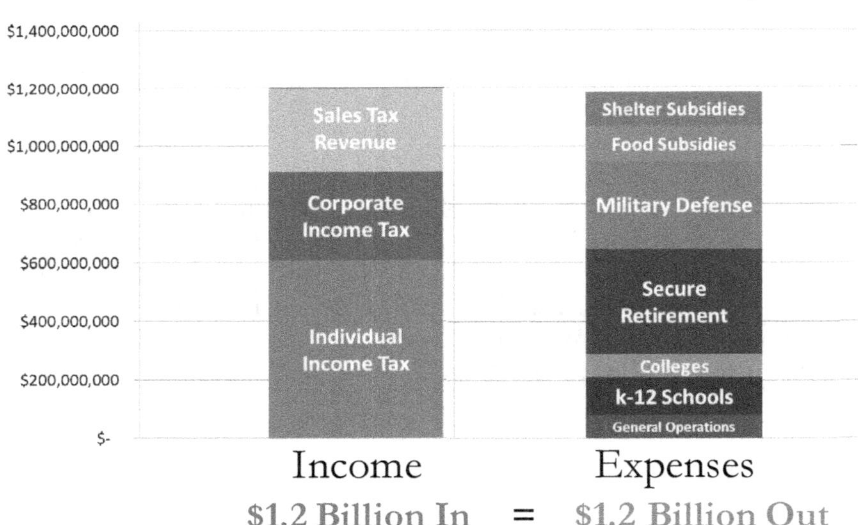

Tax Revenues are based on a flat 15% income tax rate for both individuals and companies in Trial Town. In addition, we have a sales tax equal to 5% of all sales that occur within Trial Town. Our town provides all of the basic government services you would expect, including public education, a robust college support program and military defense, which includes all local law enforcement. We also have social entitlement programs that are intended to help folks that are simply down on their luck. These programs include food and shelter subsidies for approximately 5% of Trial Town's population. In addition, Trial Town has a retirement payment plan funded out of the fifteen percent income tax for Trial Town's entire workforce. Trial Town pays a minimum retirement payment to those who have not paid into the system as well. The Secure Retirement fund pays for 10% of our population who are currently retired and over the age of 65.

Now for my story. I had always thought that we had a balanced approach to our government until one cold January morning when I decided to have coffee with a local citizen, Mary Spencer. Mary called me in mid-December and asked to meet with me about some topics of concern about our community. I told Mary that I was busy over the holidays but would be glad to meet with her in January. That time had now come and I was meeting Mary at my favorite coffee shop.

I met Mary as she was sitting at a table for two in our local coffee shop. "Hi Mary, thanks for meeting with me!"

Mary stood shaking my hand and politely responded, "Mayor, I should be thanking you for meeting with me. I've wanted to meet with you to talk about how our government can do more for its citizens."

The waitress approached our table to get our drink order. "What'll you have?" she asked.

"I'll have a plain, black coffee," I replied.

Mary said, "I'll have a Carmel Macchiato with an extra shot of espresso."

We chatted about many things that did not seem to really matter while we waited for our drinks. Our waitress quickly returned with our concoctions in hand and we anxiously sipped the hot drinks to warm ourselves from the winter chill.

"Okay, Mary," I said, "now let me better understand how Trial Town can improve the services we offer our citizens."

Mary took a quick sip of the foam on top of her drink to buy herself a little time before her response. "Mayor, Trial Town is a very prosperous town and I don't believe that all citizens are sharing in the prosperity of our town as they should."

"I'm not sure I understand, Mary. Can you be a little more specific?"

"While we have rich business owners and other wealthy individuals, there are other citizens who are going without basic food, housing and other necessities of human life."

"Mary, I'm still confused. We do have welfare and food stamp programs and even a retirement plan for all of Trial Town's citizens. What could we possibly be missing?"

"Rather than coming right out with any specific government services, I want to share a few stories of local citizens with you to better illustrate their predicament."

I took another sip of my coffee and responded, "Sure, go ahead."

"My first story is about Jane Sanchez, a 70-year-old old senior citizen who is on Trial Town's meager monthly retirement subsidy. I met Jane in a hospital emergency room a while back and she was having pains that she could not explain. I was sitting with Jane when the doctor told her that she had breast cancer. Jane was in tears as she told me that she didn't have health insurance so she didn't know how she could do anything about the problem. Mayor, Trial Town needs to create some program that can help people like Jane Sanchez when they find themselves in these situations."

Admittedly, I was tearing up as I listened to Mary tell Jane's story. "I could not agree with you more. Were you thinking that Trial Town should provide some kind of government health insurance program for our citizens who have reached retirement age?"

Mary replied, "Mayor, I am so glad you see the problem. Yes, I think government health coverage would help people like Jane. However, I have a few more stories that may expand your thinking about other services that Trial Town should be providing its citizens."

"Go ahead; I'd like to hear more."

"My next story is about Frank Fulton. Frank is part of our working class and makes about $30,000 per year. However, his employer doesn't offer health care coverage for its employees. I didn't experience that same heart-wrenching feeling as I did with Jane, but Frank could easily be caught off guard by a medical condition that he couldn't possibly afford."

"I can certainly see that, Mary. I'm fortunate that Trial Town pays for my health insurance, but I'm concerned about those people like Frank who can't afford the medical care they need."

"Mayor," Mary implored, "I really think that we need a comprehensive health care program that can cover anyone that has somehow been missed by whatever current systems we have in place."

I replied, "Mary, I'll certainly keep this in mind. Any other stories?"

Mary quickly responded, "I have a few more stories. My next story is about a natural disaster that we had just last year. As you know, the flood that came through Trial Town caused damage to the properties of many Trial Town citizens. Although Trial Town did come up with funds to make repairs to streets, schools and government facilities, there was no financial help for local merchants or residents who couldn't afford to make repairs to their buildings. My specific story is about Jim Jenkins. Jim is a hardware store owner on Main Street. His store suffered major flood damage, to the tune of $30,000. Jim didn't have the funds to make repairs so he had to borrow money. I believe that these costs will be reflected in higher costs at Jim's store. But if his prices are too high, he may go out of business."

"So, Mary, are you thinking about some sort of emergency help fund that we can give to citizens of Trial Town that suffer damage?"

Mary said, "Mayor, you and I are definitely on the same page. I do have one more story about a local farmer."

I responded, "Please continue."

Mary took a sip of her drink and then continued. "I'm sure you know one of our largest farmers in the community, Ben Chadwick. Ben farms wheat that he sells to the three bread-making companies in our town. Ben told me that he can't charge enough to keep his farms operating and is considering closing his farms. If Ben closes his farms, he will lay off close to 1,000 employees and all wheat will have to be purchased from Capital City farmers. I believe if Trial Town can step in and give Ben $1.00 per bushel of wheat produced, this will be enough to keep Ben's farm in business and keep these jobs within Trial Town."

"I had no idea Ben was thinking of closing down his farms. It sounds like this could have a bigger negative impact on Trial Town than I thought."

Mary responded, "Mayor, I'm glad that I could enlighten you on these topics. There's just one more idea that I wanted to share with you."

As I looked at the bottom of my empty coffee cup, I said, "Please continue, Mary."

"Along the same lines of helping Ben stay in business in Trial Town, I thought it would be a good idea to provide incentives to companies to move into Trial Town. As you know, Trial Town's tax revenues will increase with more local jobs and the added sales tax revenues from new companies in our community. I believe Trial Town ought to offer a refund of all sales tax for new companies starting up their business in Trial Town for their first three years of business."

I remarked, "Mary, that's simply a brilliant idea. I think this will be a win-win for Trial Town. We will attract new companies, grow our tax base and provide jobs for Trial Town citizens. That's simply a brilliant idea!"

Mary continued to share with me thoughts about many other gaps in our government including: alcoholic recovery programs, battered women's shelters, single mom assistant programs, recreation programs, community bike and walking trails, a program to manage fish and wildlife for our town, a department of environmental management, an energy department and multiple intelligence gathering organizations to prevent surprise attacks from unfriendly countries.

We finally closed our meeting.

Mary was smiling from ear to ear. "Mayor, I'm so glad that you have given me this time to bend your ear. It really does sound like we are like-minded about these concerns. I'm eager to see what actions you are able to implement in the next few years."

"Mary thanks for the meeting. I will take all of these items seriously and speak with my city council and adopt government programs to address your concerns."

We both left the coffee shop that day with a sense of mission. I was particularly moved by our conversation. I had always felt Trial Town was a great place to live and work; but now I knew there were some glaring gaps we had to fill to make life in our town perfect.

I initially thought all of the programs Mary had requested might cost too much for our town to bear. However, after I had my staff run some numbers, I put together a budget that I thought could actually work. I was so excited to present my plan to the city council.

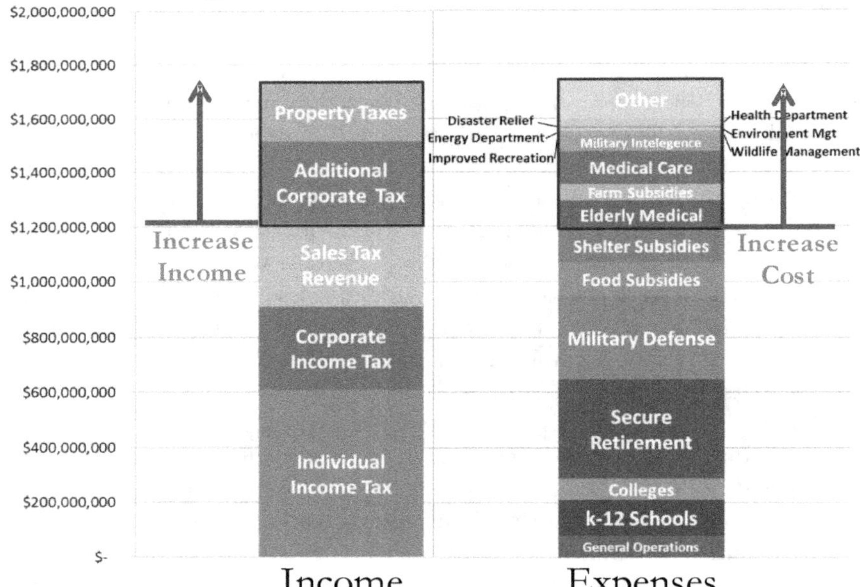

All of the additional costs would certainly increase the cost of running Trial Town. However, I believed the cost increases were only about 50% of our existing budget. I also believed that we could easily double our corporate tax rate. After all, corporations in Trial Town don't vote so they couldn't directly oppose the tax increase. I also felt it was high time that Trial Town started charging property taxes. After all, once we had implemented all of these great community programs, Trial Town would be the best place to live in the entire world.

I was very ready to present my ideas to our city council. I invited Mary to attend the meeting with me to share her personal stories that I felt would be compelling to our city council members.

When I presented my ideas to our city council, I got the typical negative input from a few of our members but resounding support from most members of our city council. They passed our new expanded budget, including tax and spending increases, by a vote of 4-2. Mary and I were very pleased that we could finally close any gaps and create the perfect community for Trial Town citizens.

With our newfound taxing authority, we started making the necessary announcements to those who would be required to pay the new taxes. As could be expected, I got many nasty calls from folks that would be paying higher taxes. I had no illusions; I knew that some in our community would have to go without some luxuries so that others in our community could live respectable lives.

Sure enough six months after we had implemented the tax increases, revenues started coming in and we were initiating our government programs that would eventually make Trial Town one of the best towns in the world. I could just see the awards and recognition rolling in from all over.

The first year involved several hiring and administrative changes. We had to build several new government buildings to house all of the new departments. At first, we had to advertise all of our new programs so that people would actually use these services. It took a few years for us to get the word out about all of the new government services being offered by Trial Town. After the third year of the programs being in place, it seemed that many citizens were taking advantage of these newly offered services.

Just as I had hoped, I did receive accolades from fellow mayors around the nation. I have two shining plaques hanging on my wall in recognition of developing one of the best government programs in the United States.

I was sitting at my desk admiring my plaques. I thought to myself, "Trial Town will be able to demonstrate to all governments that you can offer comprehensive government services within a sustainable budget

As I was daydreaming about our grand town, Sammy Penbrook poked his head in. "Mayor, do you have a few minutes?"

"Sammy, I have all the time in the world for you. Please come in," I replied.

As usual, Sammy had his charts, tables and graphs that he seemed to carry with him everywhere. Sammy laid out a very simple chart showing how our population had changed since we had added many of our needed government programs.

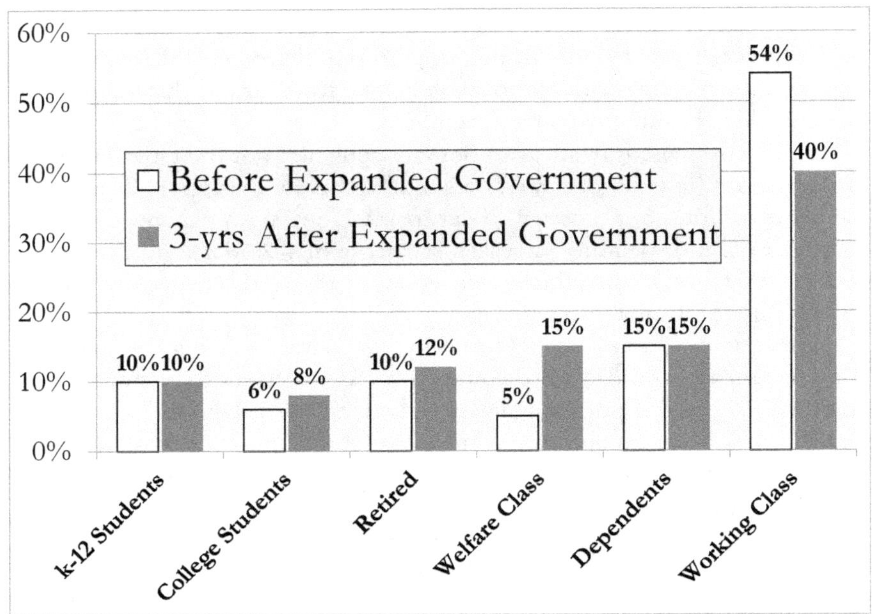

Sammy started his rant. "Trial Town has seen a dramatic shift from our working class to our welfare and college class. The word on the street is that many who were working felt it might be easier to stop trying to make a living on a low wage job and take welfare instead. I have also noticed an increase in our population, the result of an influx of other folks who feel Trial Town's welfare system is much more attractive than that of neighboring towns. Some of the workers took advantage of our college assistance program and decided to go back to school, and have shifted to the College Student category."

"Okay, I guess that should've been expected to some extent. When you have one of the best communities in the world that takes care of their own, people will want to move here," I responded.

"Mayor, I'm not sure if you understand the seriousness of this problem. In addition to the shift in our population, 30% of Trial Town's most productive companies have left our town and started manufacturing their goods in Capital City."

"How can we be losing companies with all of the sales tax subsidies we are giving?"

"The sales tax incentive was only for incoming companies, not existing companies that currently reside in Trial Town. Ironically, these companies were given sales tax incentives to move to Capital City. Plus they could continue to pay a lower corporate tax rate of 15% in Capital City. The net result is that even though we increased our tax rate from 15% to 30%, only half of the companies remained in Trial Town, resulting in no change in incoming corporate tax revenue."

I was worried: a population shift plus large companies leaving our community. I asked Sammy, "Okay. I know you have it in that stack of papers. What does our budget look like for this coming year?"

Expand Government Plan Expenses

Budget vs Actual (After 3-yrs)

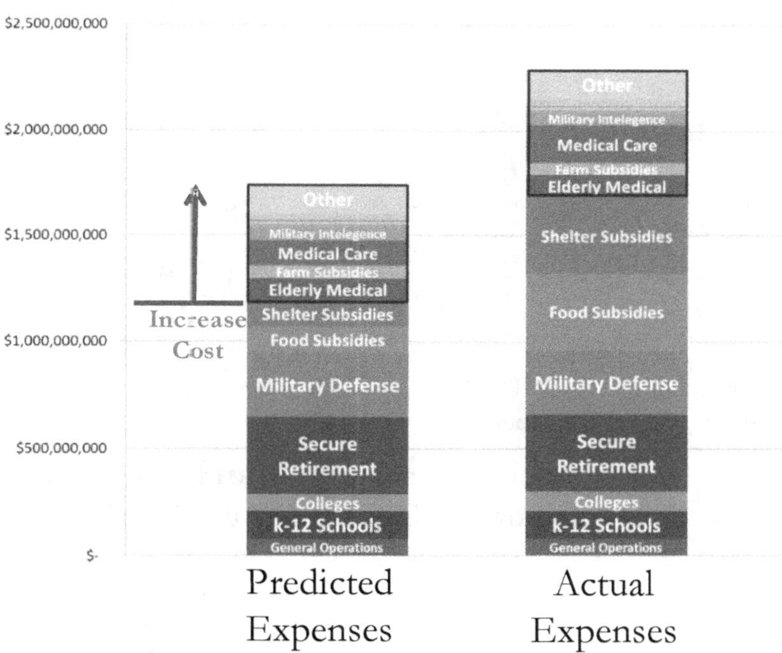

Sammy said, "Here are the final results for last year. The good news is that we managed to stay within spending limits for the most part on most of the programs that had been in place prior to our expansion of government. The one exception is spending on programs designed to help the less fortunate."

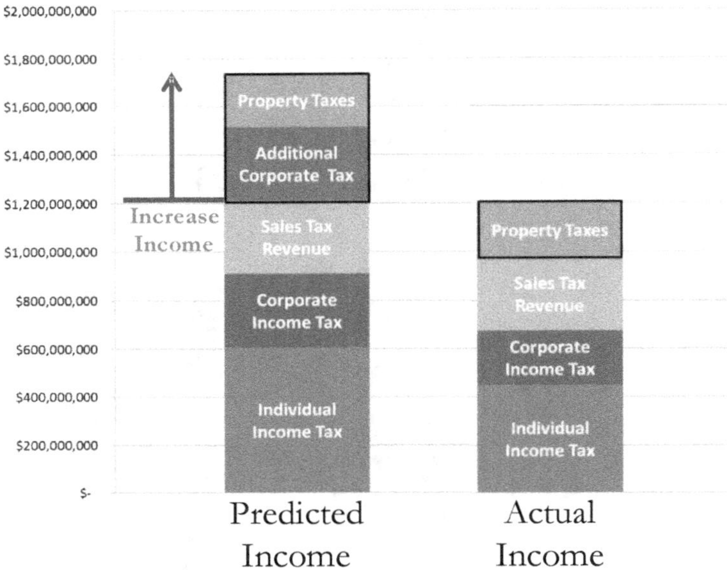

Sammy continued, "The bad news is that revenue is way down… and our expanded service expenses are way up."

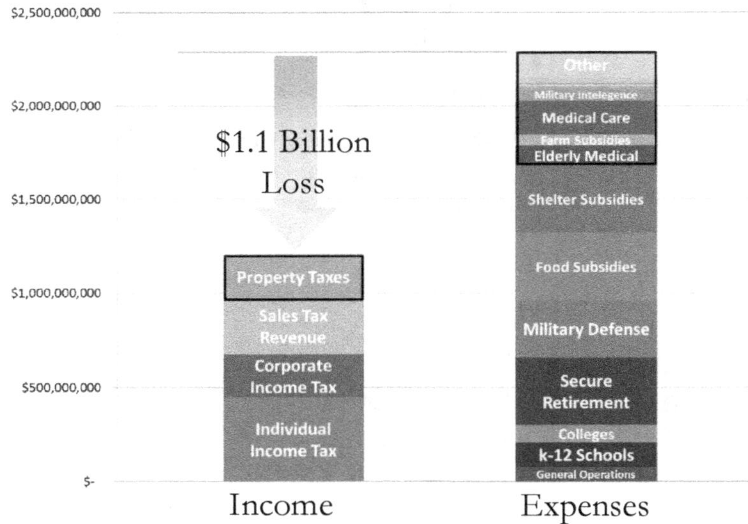

I immediately focused on the bottom line on Sammy's chart… a whopping $1.1 billion budget deficit. My heart sank. "Sammy, are you telling me that we had to borrow $1.1 billion to make sure we paid our bills this past year?"

Sammy responded, "I'm afraid so, Mayor. As you can see, there's no way we can sustain this kind of budget shortfall for even one year let alone many years after this."

"I'm sure tempted to just press Trial Town's reset button to erase this debt and all of our government services but it just seems like there should be a way to make all of this work. I'm going to meet with James Pennyworth to see what he has to say. He may be able to give me better insight into what went wrong."

Sammy responded, "Okay, boss. Just let me know if you need more information. Sorry to be the bearer of bad news."

I called James Pennyworth, whose paper mill was one of the companies that stayed in Trial Town during our most recent experiment. I did not explain all of the problems that Sammy had shared with me. I only stated that I needed help with Trial Town's budget. James seemed eager to help.

James knocked on my door. "Come in, come in, James."

James looked at the front wall of my office and commented, "Great… you have a white board. I think that can help our discussion."

"James, I don't understand how you even know what our discussion could be about."

"Arthur, you just made a move last year to expand government to try to address many gaps in government services. Then you raised corporate taxes to pay for these added services. My guess is that you are now in over your head and have probably amassed a little debt in the process. Am I right?"

I was astonished by his knowledge of our situation. "I guess that's why I invited you to this meeting." I then showed James all of the numbers that Sammy had shown me earlier.

James remarked, "Wow. This is worse than I'd anticipated."

"Okay, James, I know it's bad but I really feel people have now come to expect all of the government services that we've started offering. Is there any way we can save these services and not go bankrupt?"

"I want to take a little detour in our conversation." James then proceeded to use the white board to draw some lines that looked like the image below:

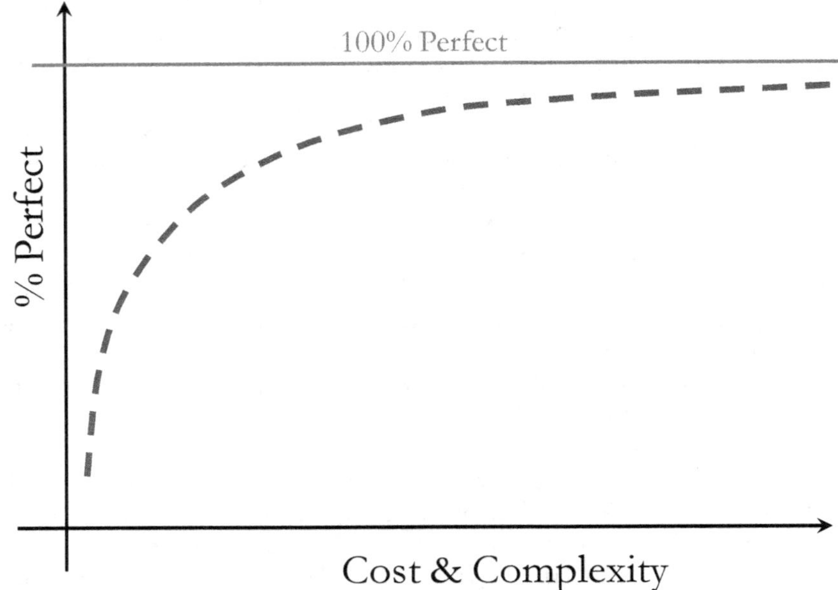

James then started talking. "I use this chart a lot of times with my business managers. In business, we understand that we have finite resources. In government you believe you have unlimited resources by simply taxing more. That's where you always go wrong."

I looked at the chart and admitted, "James, I really don't get what you're saying."

James nodded. "Okay, let's start the lesson. The left vertical axis measures perfection while the bottom horizontal axis measures cost. As you invest more costs, you are able to come closer to 100% perfection. The key lesson of this chart is that you can never reach complete perfection."

"James, I still don't understand what this has to do with our attempt to expand government services in Trial Town."

James then proceeded to draw a blue vertical line on the left side of his chart.

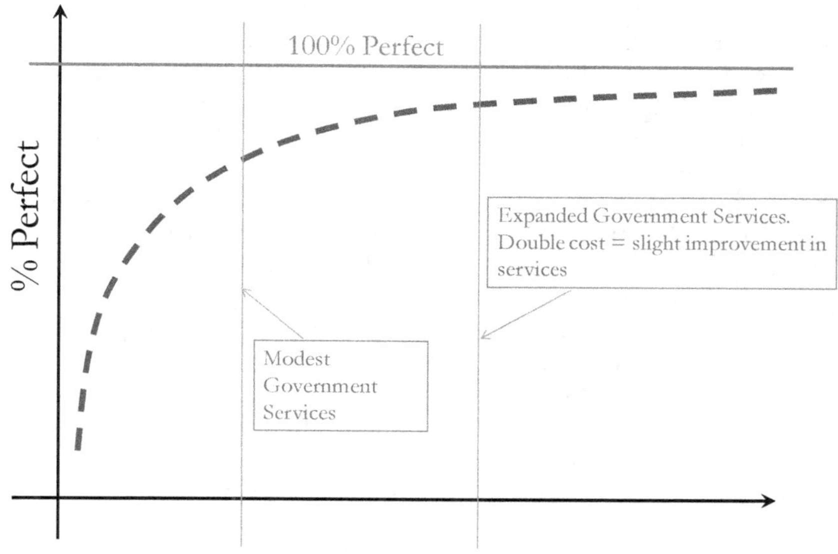

Cost & Complexity

"Arthur, Trial Town's government started at this point (James pointed to his line on the left). Then, after some discussions with community members, you felt Trial Town was lacking some government services to make it one of the best communities in the world. This represents the difference between 100% perfect at 85% perfect, which was where we were."

I then interjected, "And when we tried to expand services in our government, we made a small improvement to 95% perfect. But that increase cost us twice as much to operate our government."

James smiled. "That's exactly right. That's one concept we battle with in industry all the time. We have to make a product for a specific price. Our price has a fixed limit. We can't spend an infinite amount of money making our products perfect, so we have to figure out a creative way to improve our product with little added cost."

"James, are you saying that we may have been able to add these government services without such an increase in cost?"

"Not necessarily, Arthur. However, you have to consider your existing revenue as a hard stop. Your revenue dictates what services you can offer. After that you need to make priorities and figure out which services are most important."

"James, we thought we had a way to increase our revenue thereby funding all of the additional government services."

James continued as if I had not said a word. "You thought that you could advertise these great social support programs without some influx of welfare class people from neighboring communities. This was one of the things that increased your costs. You also increased corporate taxes, thinking that corporations could afford these taxes with the profits that they were making. However, corporations use these profits to reinvest in their businesses and rely on reasonable tax rates to make reasonable profits for reinvestment. As soon as many business owners understood that they'd be competing with Capital City companies that had lower tax rates, they quickly decided to move… taking Trial Town's tax revenues with them."

"So are you saying that we should eliminate all of the expanded government services that we added?" I asked.

"I'm not a proponent of taxes, but the property tax that you levied is probably one you can keep."

"Why can we keep this one but not any of the other increases?"

"Most surrounding communities charge property taxes and income taxes that are comparable with Trial Town. So you can levy this tax and citizens of Trial Town won't be compelled to leave as there's not a better deal in a different town."

I asked, "So which expanded government services should we keep?"

"Arthur that's more of a decision for you and your city council. You know how much you have to spend. Just don't go beyond your expenses and you should be in good shape."

After brief consideration, I asked James, "If Trial Town increased the tax rate and total tax revenues went down, will we make more money if we reduce tax rates below their previous levels?"

James smiled. "As I mentioned, Arthur, I'm not a fan of taxes, but I'm aware that the government needs some funds to operate needed services."

James then drew another chart on the whiteboard. It was an upside down red dashed line curve with several blue lines. He then spoke as he added some descriptions. As he wrote on the right side of the chart, he said, "If tax rates are too low, Trial Town will not be able to collect sufficient revenues to operate basic government services."

"But you just lectured me on the danger of high tax rates. You stated that if we raise taxes, companies will leave Trial Town."

"Yes, that is correct. But if you have a low tax rate, you will still not get much revenue for the town."

"Okay, I get it. A small percentage multiplied by a large amount of companies is still a low number."

Then James pointed to the right side of the chart. "If you raise taxes too high above this reasonable level, Trial Town will lose revenue. Companies will either leave town for a lower tax rate elsewhere or wealthy folks will decide to invest their wealth in other endeavors that are not as risky."

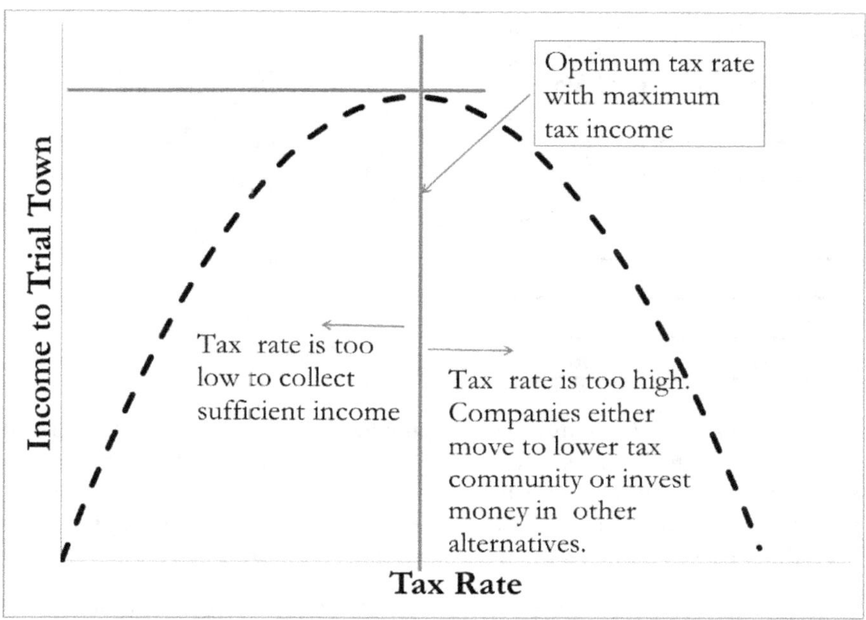

I walked up to the white board and pointed to the top of the curve. "So you are saying that there is an optimum tax rate where Trial Town can maximize its total tax revenue. What tax rate is that for us?"

"Arthur, before your corporate tax increase, Trial Town had a flat income tax rate of 15%. That's comparable to tax rates in Capital City and other adjacent communities. Like I said before, you can probably keep your property tax but will need to back off on your additional corporate taxes."

"Thank you so much for your wisdom, James. I think I know what I need to do."

"I'm glad I could help. Good luck!"

After James left, I reviewed my list of budget line items. I started with welfare and social programs. It seemed that a big variable that determines our financial strength as a community is attracting working class folks. With generous welfare programs, we are giving current workers less incentive to stay employed and we are attracting welfare class folks from neighboring communities. As I interviewed neighboring mayors, they indicated to me that they had work requirements for welfare and would only allow a maximum of two years on welfare. I felt this was fair and so Trial Town would establish similar requirements for our welfare program.

After my discussion with James, it was an easy decision to rescind the increased corporate income tax but leave the property tax in place as it was not a tax that was higher than any neighboring community.

Based on these two changes, I felt we could get our population back to the percentages in the table below:

Life Status	% Pop
k-12 Students	10%
College Students	6%
Retired	11%
Welfare Class	6%
Dependents	15%
Working Class	52%
TOTAL	**100%**

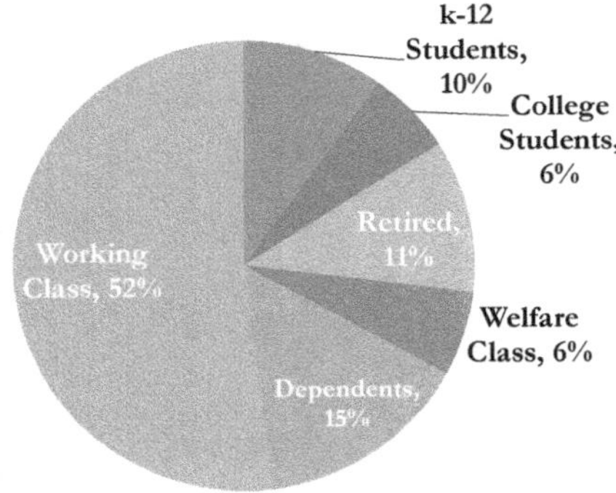

As I re-calculated the numbers, I still needed to trim several programs to get our budget to balance. I felt elderly medical care should be a priority. I also felt our expanded recreation programs were quite popular with our community members and so I kept these as well. I ended up cutting most everything else to come to the budget summary shown below.

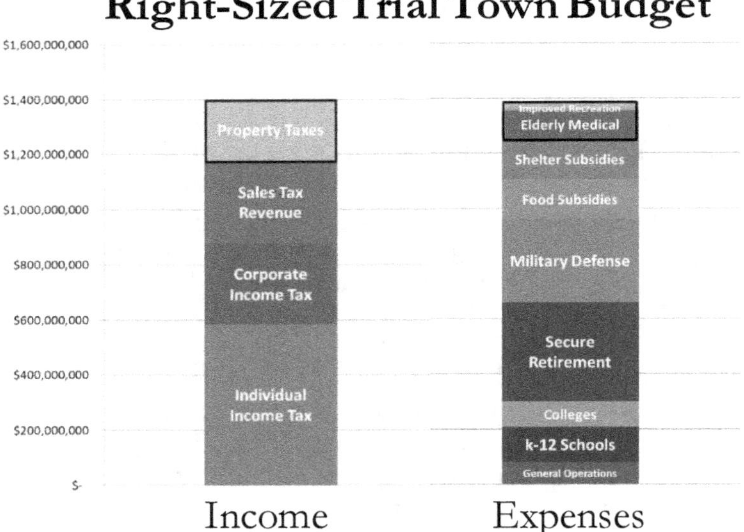

$1.4 Billion In = $1.4 Billion Out

I was now ready to present my findings and recommendations to the city council to get their blessing on our new plan. As I entered our city council room, I noticed Mary Spencer sitting in the audience. I remembered how Mary and I were so excited about our new expanded government plan and I could only imagine how she would react to my presentation today.

Nevertheless, I gave almost the same lecture to the city council as the lecture James gave me only a few days earlier. I conveyed how our efforts to expand government and raise taxes were a financial failure. I communicated our limitations on tax increases. I explained that the tax environment with neighboring communities would attract businesses and working class citizens away from Trial Town. I then went on to discuss how we had inadvertently attracted additional welfare class folks from neighboring communities and how this negatively affected some ratios that created a $1.1 billion deficit in our annual budget.

The city council was nodding in understanding as I went through the logic of why the expanded government plan was failing financially. I noticed Mary getting angrier and angrier at every word that came from my mouth.

It is customary to have any community members weigh in before the city council makes any final decisions in our council meetings. This evening was no different.

I offered, "I'd like to invite anyone in our community to weigh in on this important conversation for Trial Town."

As expected, Mary stepped up to the podium. "I'd like to voice my disappointment in you, Mayor… and my disappointment in this city council for giving up so easily on supporting these needed community services."

I then responded, "Mary, I was quite hopeful about these expanded government services as you know. Do you have any recommendations to make these services financially viable?"

"I think we can ask for more tax increases to help fund these needed programs."

"Mary, it's apparent that we can only increase taxes to the point that is equal or below our neighboring communities without losing our companies and working class folks, who are needed to fund our government."

Mary was furious. "I just cannot believe how you all have let us down. We had great government services that will now be cut off. I can tell you there will be many hopping mad folks that won't like this one bit."

Our city council voted 4-2 to approve my new budget plan as proposed. After the meeting, I pressed the reset button on our town to set things back to the way they were before our expanded government approach. Trial Town then proceeded with my new budget plan.

As predicted, our population leveled out to have a majority working class and we had a balanced budget once again. I would see Mary on occasion after this incident and it was always difficult. I had really hoped to accomplish all of the things I felt were possible with our expanded government plan. However, reality taught me a valuable lesson that I will never forget. You can only spend what you can collect. Any more spending will result in unsustainable debt. I also learned that welfare programs could pull people out of gainful employment and become a constant expectation of income for those that do not work if not administered properly. I hope that Mary can see the wisdom of these decisions someday.

Real World Examples

The United States has been embroiled in this problem for the past four decades. Congress cannot decide what programs to cut. Republicans seem to like military spending, foreign aid, and tax breaks for churches. Democrats are attached to social entitlement programs, green energy, and public education. Ironically, instead of letting go of lower priority programs, Democrats and Republicans agree to support additional spending on their opponent's projects only if their opponent agrees to spend more on their pet projects. This is like a family that cannot afford a new car but if the husband agrees to allow his wife to buy a new car, he can also buy the new car. As you can imagine, the family cannot survive financially with this kind of logic. Nor can our government.

Over the past four decades, our federal government has amassed $18.5 trillion in debt because of our government's inability to cut unnecessary federal spending and/or raise sufficient revenue to pay for that spending. If you add the unfunded future liabilities of Social Security, Medicaid and Medicare, this number is closer to $100 trillion. A mandatory spending cutting program had taken effect on March 2013 called, 'The Sequester'. This program required congress to reduce costs by 10% on all federal spending programs. Congress and the administration have found ways around many of the Sequester cuts. They have also levied tax increases for high-income earners and added healthcare taxes in an attempt to balance the budget.

A budget deficit is defined as an annual amount that the government spends over what it takes in for that year. Budget deficits for the United States have been declining from $1 trillion/year in 2009 to$500 billion in 2015. This slow progress will not get us to a point of financial solvency unless taxes are increased in areas that make sense, and/or spending is cut in areas that make sense. Since many middle income Americans already pay close to 50% of their income in taxes and public fees, it is likely that we are already beyond the optimum tax rate on the curve shown for Trial Town. The two options left are to: 1) dramatically cut unneeded spending; and 2) eliminate tax loopholes.

5 A PERFECT UNION

"All government employees should realize that the process of collective bargaining, as usually understood, cannot be transplanted into the public service."
—Franklin Delano Roosevelt

In Trial Town, the city council also acts as the school board for Trial Town Schools. Many of the teachers working for Trial Town Schools were convinced they were not being paid a fair wage. This feeling was further promoted by the national teacher's union Teachers Together. Teachers Together posted several advertisements around all of the schools, inviting teachers to a meeting to decide if they wanted to organize into a union.

The meeting was to be held at the Trial Town High School gym at 7:00 p.m. on Saturday evening. Sarah White, George Falstaff and Laura Snell all showed up early to get a seat near the front of the gym.

Sarah White taught the third grade at Trial Town Elementary School. She was not happy with her current salary and believed that a teacher's union could certainly help better negotiate compensation with collective bargaining.

George Falstaff was a teacher of the second grade at Trial Town Elementary School. George was also somewhat displeased with the general condition of his classroom. It seemed his classroom would overheat in the fall and spring; and it would be too cold most of the winter. Although George felt a union could offer some benefits, he believed that the current school district administration was doing all they could with the funds they had available. He also had a bad experience with a teacher's union in Capital City where he used to teach.

Laura Snell taught the sixth grade at Trial Town Elementary School. Laura was not pro-union or anti-union. She was attending the meeting because she was simply curious to hear what the union could do for teachers in their district.

Sarah approached George at the entry to the gym while he was talking to Laura. "Great to see you here, George. I would've guessed that you would be against unionizing teachers."

"Why do you say that, Sarah?"

Laura then chimed in. "George, you are always telling us how unions cost a lot and really don't get you much for your money."

George responded, "Well ladies, I want to know what's going on, just like everyone else in this gymnasium. If nothing else, maybe I can ask some important questions that help prevent both of you from making the wrong decision."

Their discussions continued until they heard the union leader, Kenneth Kline, call the meeting to order. Kenneth was sitting at a table with four other union folks on the stage.

Kenneth spoke with a very professional and fluid voice. You could tell he had made this same presentation several times to other school districts in the recent past. His presentation was well rehearsed and all of the teachers in the gym were hanging on his every word. Kenneth's main points in his presentation communicated how teachers in unionized school districts:

1) are paid more than teachers in this district;
2) have better benefits;
3) have a voice in political discussions;
4) have a formal voice in negotiations with city council members;
5) have a much lower teacher turn-over rate;
6) have tenure programs; and
7) are happier than non-union school districts.

After 30-minutes of presenting slides, the lights in the gym were turned back on. It was now time for questions and answers. Once the question and answer session concluded, the teachers of Trial Town Schools would vote to decide if they would unionize.

George Falstaff was the first teacher to raise his hand to ask a question. Kenneth called on George. "So you say that we can expect to get higher salaries if we unionize. How much should we expect to get in a salary increase?"

Kenneth answered, "As I mentioned in my presentation, union teachers typically make 10% more than non-union teachers."

George remained standing and quickly spoke back. "I appreciate your presentation, but I'd like to know exactly what teachers who work for Trial Town Schools can expect as an increase."

Kenneth was noticeably shaken. "Your specific situation will depend on your current salaries and how successful we are at negotiating salary increases. I can say that we should be able to get all of you increases."

George then quickly got the last word in. "So what you are saying is that you cannot guarantee any of us salary increases. Thank you." George quickly sat down, leaving a frowning Kenneth on the stage.

Sarah White raised her hand. Kenneth called on her. Sarah said, "Currently Trial Town Schools gives bonuses to teachers who graduate a class that gets an overall "Exceeds Expectations" on Trial Town's education standards test. Will this bonus continue if we unionize?"

Kenneth smiled. "The Trial Town School District is probably just holding back compensation for those who don't achieve this target for whatever reason. Within a union, we will ensure that you ALL benefit from such available compensation."

Sarah White responded with a humble thank you as she sat back down.

George Falstaff raised his hand again and was called on by Kenneth. "How much money in union dues will be taken out of our paycheck?"

Kenneth answered, "Your union dues will be $75 per month. I guarantee you will all see a lot of value for your dues in the benefits we will ultimately negotiate for you all."

George again remained standing. "I have another quick question. If we vote to unionize, can individual teachers opt out of the union?"

Kenneth smiled as he responded, "The purpose of a union is to have collective bargaining power with your school board, or, in Trial Town's case, its city council. If individual members decide to get benefits of the bargaining power of the union but do not pay union dues, it's not fair to the majority of teachers in the union. So, to answer your question, no. If you vote to approve unionization, you will all be members of the union and you will all benefit from our contract negotiations."

Many other such questions were posed, ranging from compensation, benefits, working conditions and many other teacher concerns. Kenneth was quite good at painting a very positive picture for the unionization of teachers at Trial Town Schools.

After a moment of silence, Kenneth said, "We have made a presentation of the benefits of unionization. We have answered all your questions. I believe unionization would help you all in compensation, benefits and general working conditions. It's now time to vote. You will notice that you have a simple voting ballot card on your chair. Please fill out the card and designate your vote, yes or no. We will count the votes tonight to learn what you all have decided as teachers."

Every teacher who attended dropped his or her completed ballot in the ballot box at the front of the gym. After the voting was completed, the ballots were counted. The Trial Town School District was comprised of approximately 530 teachers. Four-hundred teachers attended the meeting. After the votes were counted, the teachers that voted decided to approve the unionization by 250 to 150.

The union then held elections for local representatives from amongst the Trial Town School's teachers. Tom Gavin, a seventh grade teacher at Trial Town Junior High, was elected as the key union representative to represent teachers in negotiations with the city council.

The first realization that all teachers were unionized was the deduction of the union dues in their next paycheck.

I was called by Tom Gavin to discuss the unionization of Trial Town Schools. We met at my typical favorite meeting place, Pirate's Cove Restaurant.

Tom started our conversation. "Thanks for meeting with me, Mayor."

"I'm glad to meet with you, Tom. Honestly, I'm not sure what all of this union stuff means as this is my first experience with unions."

Tom tried to explain. "Well, Mayor, us teachers feel the city has not exactly treated us that well in our compensation, benefits and general working conditions. That's why we voted to approve unionization of all teachers in Trial Town Schools. This way we feel we'll have a collective voice to negotiate these items with you and the city council."

I was a little disappointed. "Tom, I feel Trial Town has treated teachers fairly over the years. We got a lot of positive feedback from many of the teachers that received bonus checks when their class achieved "Exceed Expectations" in our standard testing results."

Tom responded, "You've certainly done what you can for us teachers but we voted to approve unionization because we feel that you can do better."

"Okay. So do you have any specific requests that should be presented to our city council for consideration?"

The blood drained from Tom's face as this question had caught him off guard. "Mayor, I don't have anything specific at this point. I need to meet with our teachers to get a list of their priorities. My sense is that teachers will want higher compensation across the board."

"Okay. Once you get a list of issues, please get back to me so that we can try to get some of your needs addressed."

Tom and Teachers Together officials set up another union meeting in the Trial Town High School gym to get a list of grievances and desires. This meeting was not as well attended as the first meeting where teachers voted to decide if they wanted to unionize. Two hundred fifty teachers showed up for this second union meeting.

After a lot of discussion, the top issues that emerged from the meeting were:

- a 10% raise for teachers across the board in compensation;
- healthcare benefits that did not require the current $20 co-pay for doctor visits, and
- five non-school days in the school season that would be allowed for teacher's work days.

There were other requests like free lunches for teachers; increased parking spots; more vacation days during the school season; and an additional dental plan. These other items would have to wait for a second negotiation. For now, Tom Gavin felt he was well armed for another discussion with Trial Town's city council.

Again, Tom and I met at the Pirate's Cove to discuss the teacher's union requests.

Tom listed his issues. "Mayor, I now have a list of requests from our teachers. I believe this is a list of high priority items that we would like to include in next year's teacher's contracts."

Tom then gave me a single sheet that listed the following items:

1) Ten percent increase in compensation for all Trial Town School teachers.

2) Elimination of $20 co-pay for doctor's visits in the healthcare program.

3) Five teacher's workdays within the school year where there will be no school.

I responded, "Tom, you have implied that there may be additional requests. It may help the city council and me evaluate all of these requests at the same time so that we can see how these requests may change the Trial Town Schools' budget."

Tom again looked a little like he was caught off guard. "Mayor, we really would like to work on one thing at a time. The other requests are secondary to these initial items."

I then offered, "We have a limited budget and had planned for a raise for most teachers of 3% for next year. How will we get the money to pay for a 10% raise for teachers within our fixed budget?"

Tom quickly stated, "Mayor, all I can say is that I feel our teachers are underpaid. How you accommodate these issues is up to you and the city council."

"So, Tom, if the city council proposes a lesser alternative to these requests or votes against them, what will the teachers do?"

"Well, I guess we'd have to strike if our teachers decide that these items are critical."

"I'll seriously consider your requests and work with the city council to see if we can accommodate solutions to the needs that you have stated."

I explained all of the requests to Sammy Penbrook and asked him to meet me in the city hall conference room with a detailed list of the current Trial Town School budget. As I walked into the conference room, Sammy had the following table up on the overhead projector:

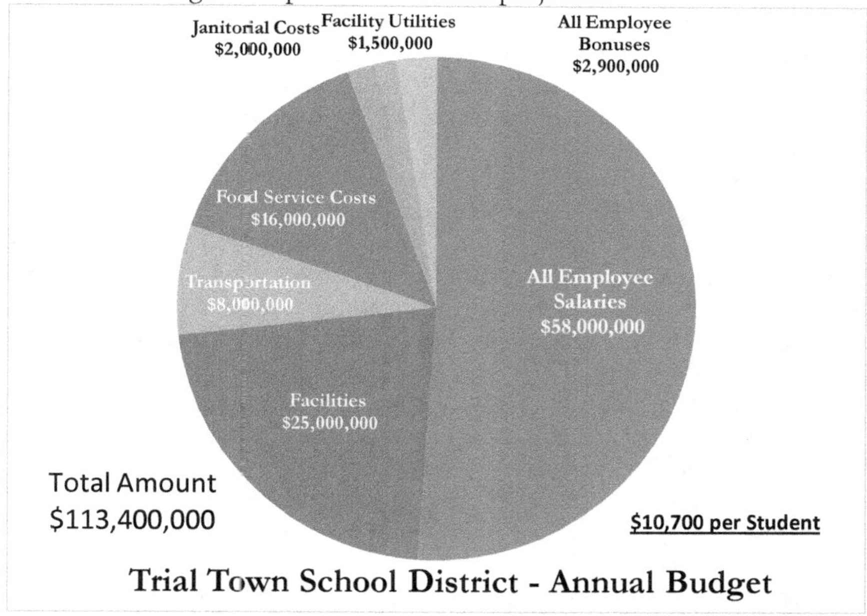

As I reviewed the amounts, I asked Sammy, "So how are we doing with our current school district budget?"

"Our spending is pretty close to our budget. We had budgeted $107,400,000 for Trial Town Schools. We are currently roughly $6 million over budget."

"So, the first request from our new teacher's union is to increase all teachers' salaries by 10%. Is there anything we can do to accommodate this request?"

Sammy thought for a while. "Well, we could eliminate the teacher's bonus program. That would give us a pay increase of 5% for teachers."

"Any other ideas to try to get to 10%?"

Sammy thought for a while. "We currently have twenty students per classroom. We can increase the student count to twenty-three students per classroom and lay off some teachers."

Sammy changed the spreadsheet and worked up the new numbers and it turned out that the district could actually reduce costs by $3 million per year by increasing teacher salaries by 10%, and cutting the $20 co-pay benefit as long as the district eliminated teacher bonuses and lay off close to seventy teachers.

"Sammy, what about the five work days per year that the teacher's union is requesting?"

"I don't think that the five work days will matter on our budget. This will just mean that the school year will be extended by five days."

"What about the energy, transportation and other costs associated with keeping the school buildings open for the additional five days?"

Sammy responded, "I really didn't think about that. I guess we could have higher facility support costs associated with the longer time. Let's estimate that at $100,000."

I met with Tom Gavin once again to present the plan to increase teacher's salaries and eliminate the $20 co-pay.

I started our conversation. "Tom, our plan is to lay off seventy teachers, which will increase classroom size from twenty students to twenty-three students. We will also have to eliminate the teacher's bonus program. Overall, I think we can accommodate all of your requests within our current budget. What do you think?"

Tom was slightly angry. "Mayor, on one hand, I am encouraged with the way you have tried to accommodate our plan, but I can tell you that our members will not be happy about the layoffs."

"Tom, how do you propose to eliminate layoffs?"

"How much of a raise could we give teachers if we don't lay off teachers?"

I remembered my conversation with Sammy and responded, "Well, I believe the raise would be closer to 4% instead of 10%."

"Okay. I'll get together with the union and our members and see what they want to do."

I then added, "Tom, I also have to let you know that the final plan will need to be ultimately approved by our city council to make it final. I'm guessing if our budget is not affected, most council members will be okay with our changes."

Tom then met with Kenneth from the Teachers Together union to discuss the offer made by Trial Town.

Kenneth was disappointed. "Tom, I think this is a weak offer being made by the Mayor. We can't afford to lose teacher positions… so the layoffs wouldn't be a good thing at all. When teachers get laid off, our union loses $75 per month per teacher."

Tom responded, "So what should we do?"

Kenneth smiled. "Tom, I suggest you recommend the smaller pay increase take effect immediately, along with the other benefits. We can then propose to the Mayor that we attempt to pass a tax increase to fund an additional 6% raise along with some other items."

Tom asked, "What if the tax increase doesn't pass?"

Kenneth smiled again. "Tom, Teachers Together has ways of getting tax increases to pass. If Trial Town gets this issue on the ballot, we can take care of the rest."

Tom held another union meeting with the Trial Town Teachers. Again, the meeting was located in the Trial Town High School gymnasium. Tom presented the plan just as Kenneth had requested. Several high-performing teachers were disappointed with the elimination of the teacher's bonus, as they would see a net decrease in their personal compensation even if the tax increase passed. Tom reassured all the teachers that they would all see a 10% increase once voters approved a tax increase. Teachers in the union supported the plan 230 votes to 100 votes.

Tom then set up a meeting with the city council to propose his plan. The city council was unanimous in its support. After all, the plan was cost-neutral. It would only cost more if the public voted for a tax increase. This meant that increased incoming funds would offset the pay increase, so Trial Town would not have to take funds from other city services to support the teacher's pay increase.

By the time the ballot issue was ready to go, the wording on the ballot had changed somewhat from the original list of demands. The ballot was worded to request an increase for teacher's salaries, funds for classroom technology upgrades and dental benefits. The total tax increase would amount to an increase of $124 per year per household. The ballot issue and campaign would be underway in the next three months to get approval by Trial Town voters.

In the meantime, several high-performing teachers decided to send their resumes to Capital City Schools and other private schools to see if they had any openings. Half of these teachers got job offers right away. Trial Town Schools replaced these teachers with other teachers who were looking for work. Ironically, some of the newly hired replacement teachers were from Capital City Schools.

What followed was quite amazing. Teachers Together started pouring money into a campaign to approve the tax increase. Teachers Together invested a total of $800,000 to support the Vote Yes campaign. Of this amount, $200,000 was directly from dues paid by teachers, with the remaining $600,000 raised from other organizations outside the Trial Town community.

The advertising campaign to approve this tax increase was more impressive than any campaign I had ever witnessed in Trial Town. Posters, radio, television, social media. They had covered all the bases. The campaign must have been worth it, because the tax initiative passed 60% YES to 40% NO.

After the passage of the tax increase, the Trial Town Schools' budget had increased by $7,000,000 per year.

Tom and the union officials set up another teacher's meeting at the Trial Town High School to celebrate the great success. This meeting was packed and there was an air of success and celebration. There was one person not celebrating. George Falstaff was handing out a single page brochure that showed a different picture than what was portrayed by Teachers Together. The key item on the paper was the table shown below.

Actual Benefits	Annual Amt	
Pay increase	$	1,723,680
CoPay Benefit	$	286,000
Dental Plan	$	1,770,912
Bonus Loss	$	(2,000,000)
Union Dues	$	(478,800)
Net Benefit	**$**	**1,301,792**

The reality is that the pay increase was not even as much as the bonus amounts that they had given up. The co-pay benefit was about what was expected. The Dental Plan was not considered a great benefit by most teachers. The other highlight that was bothersome was the amount of money paid in union dues. Many of the teachers were also aware that $800,000 was invested in the passage of this tax increase. This large cost would have to be paid back at some point.

Somehow, George managed to get a microphone at the front of the gym as everyone was celebrating and just talking amongst themselves. His voice was distinct as it came over the loud speakers. "TEST, TEST, TEST."

The crowd quieted down for the most part.

"My name is George Falstaff and I'm a teacher at Trial Town Elementary School. I first want to congratulate all of you who feel you have achieved a win in with this tax increase."

The crowd of teachers erupted in applause at George's statement.

George continued, "I've been handing out a sheet of paper that most of you now have. If you'd like one, I have extra copies. On this paper you'll see that we really didn't get much out of this effort."

The crowd of teachers got noticeably quieter and somewhat restless.

"The reality is that we gave up more in bonus compensation than we gained with our 10% raise."

A teacher in the audience interrupted by yelling out, "THAT'S GREAT FOR YOU, GEORGE, BUT MOST OF US DON'T GET BONUSES!"

George then added, "And this Dental Plan wasn't anything we desired in our original request. It was just added on once the union believed it could be successful in passing a tax increase."

The same teacher yelled out again, "GET OFF THE STAGE, GEORGE. STOP RAINING ON OUR PARADE!"

George said. "I'll get off the stage and let you all get back to your celebration. Before I do, I want to let you all know that I'm going to leave Trial Town Schools and take a job with the private school, Saddleback. If you're a high performing teacher, I suggest that you can do better elsewhere."

At this point, the same teacher yelled out again, "GET OUT OF HERE. WE'RE BETTER OFF WITHOUT YOU."

With that, George turned off the microphone and walked out of the gymnasium.

I heard about all of the activities at the union meeting and felt I needed to get a better perspective on George's viewpoint. I set up a meeting with George at the Pirate's Cove.

I started. "Thanks for meeting with me, George."

"I'm glad to talk with you about the Teachers Together union."

"So, why are you leaving Trial Town Schools?"

George answered, "Mayor, it's really simple. Many of the high-performing teachers that were making bonuses feel we just got a pay cut and so we're trying to find jobs with other schools that reward teaching excellence. So far, one hundred good teachers are planning on leaving Trial Town Schools at the end of the school year."

I was confused. "But, George, you just got a 10% pay increase, dental benefits, no doctor co-pays, and new technology in your classrooms. How can you match this someplace else?"

George smiled. "First, I made more money with the bonus system than I will now make with the 10% increase. The other benefits weren't that important to me. So I really don't value those items at all. We really didn't need new technology in our schools. We had just purchased new computers last year. "

I was a little surprised. "It kind of sounds like you're a little negative about the success the union has achieved for its members."

George responded, "Mayor, the reality is that Trial Town Schools costs $10,600 per student per year before any of the union concessions and tax increase. Now, Trial Town Schools costs $11,200 per student per year. The average cost of Capital City Schools is close to $10,000 per student per year and Capital City Schools has a teacher bonus system in place."

I still didn't get it. "So what? The higher cost per student will attract much better teachers and should improve the quality of our schools. Plus, why should you worry about the cost as long as our taxpayers seem to be okay with the cost increase?"

George laughed. "Mayor, I gave you more credit than that. Trial Town Schools is increasing its cost per student and it's inadvertently telling all teachers that they should be paid a high salary regardless of their performance. This means that high-performing teachers will leave to make more money elsewhere and mediocre teachers will be attracted to Trial Town Schools because they can make a lot of money regardless of their performance."

"Hmm, I never thought of that."

George continued. "At some point the public will get wise to the problem and understand they are paying more money for lower performance of their students and school system. Parents who can afford it will pull their kids out of Trial Town Schools and get them either to a different public school system or put them in private schools."

"That's depressing. What about the fact that the public is paying for Trial Town Schools regardless of whether their kids attend or not? Won't that compel them to keep their kids in our schools?"

"There will basically be two types of citizens: Those that can afford to pay more and really value their kid's education and simply decide to pay more elsewhere; and those that feel stuck in a substandard school system and will do whatever they can to get their old school system back."

"So are you saying that the Teachers Together has caused all of this damage?"

"The teacher's union did what unions do. They are not fully to blame. You may want to talk with James Pennyworth at the paper mill to better understand how he handles his union."

I closed our conversation. "George, I'll take your advice and talk with James. Thanks for meeting with me today."

I set up a meeting with James Pennyworth at Pirate's Cove. I did let James know that I wanted to talk to him about his union. I also indicated that I wanted to understand the difference between his union and the teacher's union.

James started our conversation. "So, Mayor, you're having union troubles."

"I don't think I'm having union problems. I had a discussion with George Falstaff and he seems to believe that the Teachers Together union will destroy Trial Town Schools."

"Why does George think that?"

"George thinks that our school district will cost too much and the quality of education will diminish. He believes Trial Town citizens will either pull their students out of the public schools, or move out of our community to find better education opportunities elsewhere."

James just smiled and took a sip of his iced tea.

"James, I was getting a sense that I did something wrong in negotiating with Teachers Together to cause these problems. How do you manage your unions at the paper mill?"

James laughed. "Arthur, you are dealing with public worker unions. I'm dealing with an industrial union. They are two different animals."

"Oh, in what way?"

"Well, first of all, when I'm negotiating with my unions, I have a genuine market restriction that I'm very aware of. I can't give any concessions that price our paper products out of the market. My union is well aware of this and is sensitive to market prices when negotiating employee benefits."

"I also communicated these budget limitations when Tom Gavin first came to me asking for pay increases."

James smiled again. "Good for you, Arthur. That was a good move on your part. However, in the public sector, unions view your budget as almost unlimited. All they have to do is pour a lot of money into a political campaign and they can manipulate the voters or political leaders to give them more benefits. In the public sector, there's no perceived 'ceiling' for costs."

"Okay, I now understand the cost ceiling problem but what about the quality of our teachers? George has indicated that he was getting a bonus that he doesn't get any more. George also indicated that his compensation has dropped in the union system. He believes that high quality teachers will leave to other schools and take students with them."

"That is another difference. Particularly between the school system and our paper mill. Paper mill employees go through a certification program that's sponsored by our union. These paper workers are highly skilled and the union has helped in developing a training program to ensure we have highly qualified paper workers. Teachers are different. They have gone to college for their basic education. Even though their education is the roughly the same, there are great teachers and bad teachers. The administrators in Trial Town Schools were aware of this difference. That is why they offered attractive bonuses to their better teachers. By treating teachers like trade workers, unions diminish the difference between high-performance and low performance teachers. This is how unions keep the majority of teachers on board with whatever programs they want to push through. High-performing teachers are usually in the minority, so their preferences never get championed by union officials."

"Wow, James! Thanks for the education on public versus private unions.

How do I undo any damage that may have been caused by the Trial Town Schools teacher's union?"

James smiled. "That's a great question. You could pass what is called "right-to-work" laws in Trial Town that allow individual teachers to opt-out of the Teachers Together union. This will most likely cut teacher union membership almost in half. This will either result in a doubling of union dues for those members who remain or result in diminished union power within the school district."

"I got a feeling I will make a lot of enemies with that move. Especially right after the recent win by the Teachers Together union."

"Your other alternative would be to try to renegotiate the teacher's contracts with the union to include bonus compensation and reduce the overall pay increase to something more modest."

I laughed. "Hell will freeze over before I can cut teacher's pay after they just got a raise."

"You're probably right."

After my meeting with James, I felt the only thing I could do was diminish the influence of the union. I was particularly concerned about teachers who didn't agree with the direction of the union. I then decided to propose and pass the right-to-work legislation that James had discussed.

I met with the city council to discuss the problems. I shared many of the points that George and James shared with me in our meetings. I was a little surprised by the reaction of the city council.

Sally Hatfield spoke up. "Mayor I was warned by some union officials that you'd try this trick."

"Sally, this is no trick. I do believe the concerns that George Falstaff described. I feel this unionization may be ultimately bad for Trial Town Schools."

"Mayor, you're simply trying to bust the Teachers Together union. This is unfair to all of those teachers who just experienced a positive win with our voting public."

I felt Sally's opposition almost seemed to be forced. I had to ask, "Sally, I don't want to pry. But have you received any financial support by the Friends of Teacher's union?"

Sally's face turned red. "Mayor, I get campaign contributions from many members of our community. Yes, I think I have gotten some contributions from the Teachers Together union. I get contributions from many others as well."

I was starting to understand. "Sally, I can always check campaign contribution records. Can you tell me how much you have received from Teachers Together?"

Sally answered, "I believe the Teachers Together has contributed about $10,000 to my campaign fund."

The rest of the council members reacted with surprise.

I then said, "Sally, thank you for your honesty. I believe I better understand your opposition on the right-to-work law."

We went ahead and took the vote on the right-to-work law and it passed 4-2. We caught a lot of flak from union officials and many other teachers. My sense is that the public never understood why we passed this legislation or the damage I felt was caused to Trial Town Schools as a result of the union presence.

Over time, the teacher union membership at Trial Town Schools dropped to around 200 members. This was not enough to allow for the type of campaigning we had seen in the recent tax increase. As George had predicted, we did suffer a loss of students and more high-performance teachers in the four years after the tax increase was approved. As the influence of the union diminished, Trial Town Schools reinstated its bonus system and stopped any pay increases to get its costs back in line with Capital City Schools. It took another 10 years for Trial Town Schools to get high-performance teachers like those that we had prior to the unionization. Nevertheless, we did make it back to education excellence in our school system.

Real World Examples

Unions have done a lot to ensure fair compensation, benefits and working conditions for many industrial workers in the United States. In addition, unions have established top-rate apprentice, journeyman, and masters programs that offer on-the-job training for trade workers. Even with these benefits, union membership in the private sector has gradually diminished over the years. This may be a cost savings measure by employees. It may also be caused by competitive pressures for companies competing on the world stage. Unions in the public sector, however, are on the rise. The largest public union is the National Education Association (NEA). The NEA is a teachers union and it has created a stranglehold on education systems nationwide. Unions that negotiate more money or benefits in a public environment can normally pressure the public or politicians to get higher tax revenues. They have the ability to influence political votes for politicians and initiatives that will funnel more funds to their members. As there are no genuine market pressures to prevent union demands from growing out of control, public officials grant these concessions with no understanding of how these costs will affect the cost and quality of government services. Many union members in both private and public unions do not agree with the actions implemented by their own unions. In many cases, union funds go to politicians who many members do not support.

These problems have led to some states passing right-to-work legislation to allow employees in unionized companies or governments to opt-out of their unions. In December 2012, the State of Michigan (a heavily unionized state) passed right-to-work legislation by a vote of the public as a measure to attempt to improve jobs and better their state economy.

The State of Wisconsin dramatically diminished the collective bargaining power of public unions in 2013 to avoid budget cost overruns. In 2015, Wisconsin passed a right-to-work statute to allow employees to opt-out of unions.

6 HEALTH CARE FOR EVERYONE

"America's health care system is neither healthy, caring, nor a system."
— Walter Cronkite

In an earlier story, you may have read about a massive government expansion that did not quite work out the way we wanted. Well, I was approached again by Mary Spencer after I felt we had right-sized the government.

Mary started the conversation. "Mayor I now understand why we couldn't offer all of the government services that we initially desired in our last effort. However, I really believe we need to do something about the problems with our health insurance in Trial Town."

"Mary, we've been down this road before. I thought that this was one of the programs we couldn't afford when we expanded many of our government services."

Mary quickly responded, "I know that we decided it wasn't affordable. I think we had the wrong approach before. Before we get too far into the numbers, I want to lay out the specific problems I see in our community."

I bit. "Okay, go ahead. But remember we have to have a solid way to pay for any fixes."

"Joe Sampson is a neighbor of mine. He was laid off from his job at the paper mill where he had great benefits. Although the paper mill would allow Joe to continue to hold his health insurance with the company after his lay off, Joe simply couldn't afford to pay the premiums without a job. Prior to Joe's layoff, he was diagnosed with a heart problem by a cardiologist at Trial Town Hospital."

"Mary, you know that we have a law in the city that Joe would have to be treated if he showed up to a hospital with any medical condition that needs attention."

"I do know that. Unfortunately, Joe's heart problem wasn't considered an emergency unless he was having a heart attack or needed immediate care to prevent death."

"So what happened?"

Mary had a tear in her eye when she responded. "Joe's heart problem got worse, creating a situation where he didn't think he could be hired by any company to do physical work. Joe felt his skills would only apply to jobs that required physical effort. He then did have a heart attack and was treated by the hospital under the Indigent Care requirement that you referenced. Joe did eventually get the healthcare that he required. But it could've cost him his life. The paper mill's business picked back up and they reinstated Joe."

"Mary, that's a sad story. It seems like things turned out okay for Joe in the end."

"That may be, but I have another story that didn't have a happy ending."

"Okay, Mary. Please continue."

"Sally Wainwright works at the homeless shelter downtown. Sally does not make much money and the homeless shelter doesn't pay for her health insurance. She had problems with her digestive system but was afraid to see a doctor because she doesn't have health insurance. Her problems didn't seem dire enough to go to the emergency room. Two months ago, Sally collapsed while she was serving food in the homeless shelter. She was rushed to the hospital. Her appendix had burst and she was pronounced dead at the hospital."

"That's a sad story. Didn't Sally have enough money just to have a doctor look at her appendix?"

Mary was sobbing. "Mayor, if Sally could have paid for the appointment, I'm sure she would have made one."

"Okay, Mary. But if we can't afford it, I'm not sure what our Trial Town government could have done to prevent either of these problems."

"Just hold on. I'll get to the payment stuff in a minute. I have one more story."

"Please continue."

"You probably know Mark Feldman."

I acknowledged that I did.

"Mark had a good job working as a manager at Trial Town Grocers. He made a lot of money but didn't get health benefits. Mark had chronic back problems all the time he worked at Trial Town Grocers. He did purchase health insurance on his own; however, each year, his insurance company would not allow any pre-existing conditions to be covered under his subsequent year's insurance policy. To make a long story short, Mark finally had a ruptured disc in his lower vertebrae and had a very expensive back surgery that cost him $120,000. Mark's insurance wouldn't cover his claim because they said his back problems were pre-existing. Mark had to wipe out his savings of $50,000 and put a second mortgage on his house to pay the balance of the cost through installment payments. Mark got his back surgery and everything worked out okay but he's financially wiped out."

"Mary, I certainly feel for Mark's predicament but I still don't see how Trial Town can help without being financially wiped out ourselves."

Mary pulled out a piece of paper with a table on it. "I have done some homework on all of the health insurance costs paid in Trial Town. Currently, our citizens and government spend approximately $932 million per year on health insurance. I have included the amount Trial Town already pays for Elderly Care. Private insurance companies claim that they pay an additional $160 million for Indigent Care, when someone shows up at the hospital who has no insurance. In these cases, hospitals have to treat the uninsured person and then charge these fees to private insurance companies. If the government administers this $160 million, I believe that we could offer actual health insurance to the poor and uninsured without spending any additional money."

I was impressed. "Mary, I'm so glad that you've done your homework. Before I make any commitments this time, I want my numbers people to review your idea."

I gave Mary's table and her back-up information to Sammy Penbrook, Trial Town's tax assessor, who has a great understanding of budgets and tax economics. Sammy expanded Mary's table and got into the actual details.

Sammy met with me in our city hall conference room to discuss some of Mary's information. He had the projector set up with a large table of numbers displayed on the projector screen.

Current Health Insurance Costs

Pop Category	P Ins	Poor	Elderly	Uninsured	Cost ($000)
Children	6.9%			3.1%	**$ 31,469**
College	4.8%			1.2%	**$ 18,881**
Retired	2.0%		8.0%	1.0%	**$ 138,462**
Poor		6.0%			**$ 54,000**
Dependents	11.9%			3.1%	**$ 135,000**
Working	41.4%			10.6%	**$ 468,000**
%	**67.0%**	**6.0%**	**8.0%**	**19.0%**	
# People	67,000	6,000	8,000	19,000	
Raw Cost ($000)	**$ 541,837**	**$ 54,000**	**$ 100,699**	**$ 149,275**	
Insurance $	$ 54,184				Government
Profit $	$ 54,184	$ -	$ (1,007)		$ 119,832
Govt OH $		$ -	$ 20,140		Private
Ind Care $	$ 162,367				$ 812,572
TOTAL Cost ($00(	**$ 812,572**		**$ 119,832**		**$ 932,404**

"Hi Sammy," I said as I walked into the conference room.

"Hi, boss."

"What is this table we're looking at?" I asked.

Sammy took a deep breath. "I'm glad you asked. This table is just a more detailed table of the one that Mary had shown you earlier. If you look at our current demographics, you can see that the majority of our population is covered by Private Insurance. This is mainly insurance that is partially or wholly paid for by employers. You can also see that we are paying for the Elderly through Trial Town's funds."

I noticed some additional numbers. "Sammy, what are these additional columns called Insurance $, Government $, Profit $, and Ind Care $?"

"Great questions. Insurance $ is the amount of money required by insurance companies in order to administer private insurance programs. I've tracked cost separately, just to see if it makes a difference in my evaluations."

I had to interrupt. "So you're saying that 10% of all health care costs are going to the insurance companies?"

"Yes. That's exactly right. Insurance companies are just like any other company. They require payment to cover their costs, risk and any profit requirements."

"It seems like we could save even more money if we cut out insurance companies altogether."

"Mayor, I'll explain why you may change your mind with my explanation of the rest of these cost items. The Government $ are the funds required by Trial Town to support any government-based insurance programs. You can see that it's costing Trial Town close to $20 million just to administer our current Elderly Care program."

"So you are saying that Trial Town is charging 20% of health care costs for the programs we are administering?"

Sammy smiled. "You got it, Mayor. You thought 10% was high but it's costing us double that to administer government healthcare programs."

I had to ask. "Why does it cost us twice as much as insurance companies?"

"This is a typical problem with government programs. Government doesn't have a profit motive. This seems to be reflected in how motivated our folks are at performing the same work as cost effectively as folks in the private sector."

I nodded and asked Sammy to continue his explanation of the other terms.

"Profit $ is the amount of profit made by the healthcare industry."

I interrupted. "There you have it! When these greedy private sector companies add in their profit, their total cost to administer health care coverage is the same as ours."

Sammy said, "Insurance and healthcare professionals take these profits and reinvest into hospitals, technology and the inventory required to operate our private healthcare system. There's no way that the healthcare system could operate at a loss, as they do with our Elderly Care program. You may notice the healthcare industry loses money on our Elderly Care program and makes money on private care."

I had to add, "They probably reinvest some of these dollars. But I'll bet investors are also taking home added income that's not being reinvested."

"You're right, Mayor. Most of these investors are common citizens of Trial Town and use this income to support their personal retirement. Without these funds, Trial Town would need to pay even more for our retirement programs."

"Okay, I got it. Profit is needed and it's a good thing to motivate the private sector to be cost efficient and reinvest in growing their business. Any funds left over are benefiting our community in other ways. Thanks for setting me straight, Sammy. Now let's get back to the rest of your table."

Sammy continued. "Ind Care $ is the amount of money that Mary was referring to that is set aside by private insurers to cover Indigent Care."

I interjected, "Is it true that Indigent Care could go away if the government pays for these folks?"

"I have talked with insurance companies and they are glad to reduce this cost in their insurance premiums if the government takes over this responsibility."

"That's a lot of money. So have you looked at how we can cover the Poor People and the Uninsured to make sure that everyone has health care coverage?"

"I have put together a plan where everyone can be covered with proactive health insurance." Sammy then switched tables to show a new table with all of the same amounts. However, the total amount had increased.

New Govt Care Health Insurance Costs (Plan)

Pop Category	P Ins	Poor	Elderly	Uninsured	
Raw Cost ($000)	**$ 541,837**	**$ 54,000**	**$ 100,699**	**$ 149,275**	
Insurance $	$ 54,184			$ 17,913	Government
Profit $	$ 54,184	$ (540)	$ (1,007)	$ 14,927	$ 412,317
Govt OH $	$ 16,255	$ 10,800	$ 20,140	$ 29,855	Private
Ind Care $	$ -				$ 650,205
TOTAL Cost ($00	**$ 666,460**	**$ 64,260**	**$ 119,832**	**$ 211,970**	**$ 1,062,522**

I reacted immediately. "Sammy, what happened? This new table shows Private Insurance going down, and Indigent Care costs going away, but there are added government costs and the total is $130 million more than the cost of our current system."

Sammy responded, "You're right. As soon as government gets involved in the administration of the insurance market place, added costs are incurred automatically across the board. I have assumed that we can try the same cost control measures on insuring the poor as we currently incur on our Elderly Plan. However, I believe insurance companies and healthcare professionals will still need to make their traditional profits as they would on private insurance."

"So are you saying that the government will have to come up with $130 million per year to fund a plan that would ensure that all citizens of Trial Town will be covered with traditional health insurance?"

"Yes. That's exactly what I'm saying."

After my meeting with Sammy, I was somewhat crestfallen, thinking that once again we couldn't afford to cover health insurance needs for all citizens of Trial Town. However, I decided to go to our city council and propose a tax increase of $2,000 per working class citizen per year so that we could cover our entire citizenry with health care insurance.

I was amazed that our city council was somewhat receptive to the healthcare tax increase with the vote being 3 to 3. This meant I had to cast the tie-breaking vote to pass the tax increase. So it was done… we drafted a new law to ensure that all citizens in Trial Town would have health insurance coverage.

I set up a meeting with Mary at our local coffee shop to discuss the great news.

"Mayor," Mary said, "I heard the great news on our local news channel. It looks like you did it."

"Mary, unfortunately, we had to pass a tax increase to fund the program. After Sammy ran some actual numbers evaluating the cost of administering the program, it turned out that we needed an additional $130 million per year to actually fund health insurance for all Trial Town citizens."

Mary raised her coffee cup. "Here's to our great mayor for finding a way to do the right thing!"

"Thanks so much. But I don't want to celebrate until I actually see it all working. We have been here before, thinking that things would work out and then disappointed when we had to reverse our stance."

It was over a year since I had met with Mary to celebrate our little success when, once again, Sammy poked his head in my office door, "I think we need to talk. Can you meet me in the conference room?"

"Sure," I said, "I'll be right in."

Sammy displayed our original financial predictions along with an actual financial performance for the healthcare program. My heart fell as I saw that the actual table showed a cost that was $180 million higher than what we had anticipated. Before Sammy could get a word out, I asked, "Sammy, what gives? Are these numbers right? We are spending $180 million more than what we had originally anticipated?"

New Govt Care Health Insurance Costs (Plan)

Pop Category	P Ins	Poor	Elderly	Uninsured	
Raw Cost ($000)	$ 541,837	$ 54,000	$ 100,699	$ 149,275	
Insurance $	$ 54,184			$ 17,913	Government
Profit $	$ 54,184	$ (540)	$ (1,007)	$ 14,927	$ 412,317
Govt OH $	$ 16,255	$ 10,800	$ 20,140	$ 29,855	Private
Ind Care $	$ -				$ 650,205
TOTAL Cost ($000	$ 666,460	$ 64,260	$ 119,832	$ 211,970	$ 1,062,522

New Govt Care Health Insurance Costs (Actual)

Pop Category	P Ins	Poor	Elderly	Uninsured	
Raw Cost ($000)	$ 498,490	$ 62,100	$ 115,804	$ 296,288	
Insurance $	$ 49,849			$ 35,555	Government
Profit $	$ 49,849	$ (621)	$ (1,158)	$ 29,629	$ 642,749
Govt OH $	$ 14,955	$ 10,800	$ 20,140	$ 59,258	Private
Ind Care $	$ -				$ 598,188
TOTAL Cost ($000	$ 613,143	$ 72,279	$ 134,786	$ 420,729	$ 1,240,938

Sammy responded, "You got it."

"What went wrong?"

Sammy breathed a long sigh and then started talking. "Well, one thing that we didn't count on was that several employers decided to drop health insurance programs. They believed their employees would be able to get insurance through the Government Care plan.

"Almost 20% of people who were covered by employers are now being covered under the Government Care plan and this has driven up government costs. Unfortunately, other employers may join this movement as they will not want to have costs that their competitors don't have."

"Okay, I guess I didn't see that one coming. So why did costs go up in our Poor and Elderly plans? We really didn't do much with these at all."

"I talked with insurance companies and healthcare providers and they gave me some great lessons on supply and demand. When we added many more people to the healthcare market with essentially free healthcare, the demand went up substantially."

I responded, "Okay. So what? What does that have to do with the prices being charged?"

"When supply stays the same and demand goes up, prices have to increase. It is Economics 101."

I was furious. "Economics 101, my foot! These greedy healthcare providers and insurance companies are just trying to take advantage of us."

"That could be but there's really nothing we can do about it unless we demand lower prices and force providers to become more cost efficient."

"You got it, Sammy. That's how we'll control those greedy insurance companies and healthcare providers. We'll control the costs to match levels that we are getting with our Elderly and Poor programs."

After my meeting with Sammy, I proposed a revision to our Government Care plan to our city council that included price controls. This time around, it was a 4-2 vote to make the change. I really didn't understand the 'NO' votes. Who would be against controlling the profits of these greedy companies?

A year later, once again Sammy poked his head in my door. Again, he had set up a meeting in our conference room. I noticed a new table being displayed on the projector screen with much better numbers.

New Govt Care Health Insurance Costs (Actual)

Pop Category	P Ins	Poor	Elderly	Uninsured	
Raw Cost ($000)	**$ 498,490**	**$ 62,100**	**$ 115,804**	**$ 296,288**	
Insurance $	$ 49,849			$ 35,555	Government
Profit $	$ 49,849	$ (621)	$ (1,158)	$ 29,629	$ 642,749
Govt OH $	$ 14,955	$ 10,800	$ 20,140	$ 59,258	Private
Ind Care $	$ -				$ 598,188
TOTAL Cost ($000	**S 613,143**	**$ 72,279**	**$ 134,786**	**$ 420,729**	**$ 1,240,938**

Cost Control Govt Care Health Insurance Costs

Pop Category	P Ins	Poor	Elderly	Uninsured	
Raw Cost ($000)	**$ 398,792**	**$ 62,100**	**$ 115,804**	**$ 316,789**	
Insurance $	$ 39,879			$ 38,015	Government
Profit $	$ 39,879	$ (621)	$ (1,158)	$ 31,679	$ 668,869
Govt OH $	$ 11,964	$ 10,800	$ 20,140	$ 63,358	Private
Ind Care $	$ -				$ 478,551
TOTAL Cost ($000	**$ 490,514**	**$ 72,279**	**$ 134,786**	**$ 449,841**	**$ 1,147,420**

Sammy started, "I have some good news and some bad news."

"I think I can see the good news. It looks like we shaved $100 million in costs comparing this year with last year. We're certainly moving in the right direction."

Sammy agreed. "We did reduce costs. We are still $80 million a year over our original budget, but costs did go down overall."

I responded, "Then what's the bad news?"

Sammy then went into a longer diatribe. "The overall costs did go down but several more employer-supported participants got added to Government Care. This means that although overall costs are down, Trial Town is now paying $669 million per year instead of the $250 million per year that we had originally anticipated. We simply cannot afford to pick up all health insurance for all people. My sense is that private employers will continue to shed employees on their plans if the government will pick them up."

"What if we force employers to cover their own employees?"

"I think we could definitely limit the shift in coverage by making such a requirement. However, our government plan is still more attractive than traditional employer plans. We would then be forcing employers to purchase a more comprehensive insurance product at a higher price. I believe this may violate our citizen's liberty."

I was pondering what Sammy was saying.

Sammy continued, "Mayor, the problems we have are not just cost issues. After we implemented cost controls, I heard several complaints of waiting periods of over a year for needed health care. This problem has created a coverage gap that is much worse than not covering folks prior to implementing the Government Care plan."

"Let me get this straight. We're currently going into debt at the pace of $420 million per year with no end in sight. If we force employers to purchase health care coverage for their employees, you're concerned about some violation of their liberty. If we stay the current course, we'll certainly go bankrupt as a city. And, you are saying healthcare waiting lines are longer than ever? Honestly, Sammy, I think this is all bad news."

"Sorry to be the bearer of this news but it is what it is."

"Okay, Sammy, I really want us to find a way for this to work. Do you have any suggestions?"

Sammy smiled. "I'm glad you asked. I believe we have three basic problems that have led to our current predicament. First, I think we need to ensure there's a free-market-based purchasing process from consumers to health insurance providers that will tend to naturally keep prices reasonable."

I was confused. "I don't understand."

"Mayor, all things in a free-market economy will be reasonably priced if there is adequate and free competition. Let's take your personal computer. Two companies offer the same computer. Company #1 is charging $750 for the computer while Company #2 is charging $600. You would purchase the computer from Company #2 for the lower price."

"Are you suggesting that all Trial Town citizens shop for each healthcare procedure? How will they know the quality of healthcare that they are purchasing?"

Sammy quickly responded, "Mayor that's not what I'm suggesting. Please let me finish. I will get to my recommended solution."

I nodded and Sammy continued. "Second, I think you have to eliminate the motivation to move employer-paid insurance to government programs.

Trial Town has been picking up the tab to pay for insurance for folks who should be able to pay for their own insurance."

"I certainly agree with that one. Trial Town will go broke paying for all of this insurance."

"Finally, I believe that government needs to play a very small role in the healthcare marketplace to avoid negatively impacting costs of healthcare."

I had to interrupt. "Sammy, how can we improve healthcare, if Trial Town is not engaged in the solution somehow?"

"Mayor, you'd be surprised at how well things can work without government intervention."

"Sammy, you sound like you've already developed a plan. So let's hear it."

"Yes, Mayor, I have come up with a plan that I think will work. I've called this new plan the Health Marketplace Plan as it relies on free-market principles rather than government control. Here are the elements of my plan:

1) Define ten insurance plans with different features. The lowest cost plan will be a High-Deductible Plan with the basic necessities; while the highest cost plan will be a Low-Deductible Plan with a lot of coverage. We need insurance companies to help us better define the specific coverage included with each of these plans.

2) Prequalify insurance companies to participate in Trial Town's market place. Insurance companies will need to have experience with administration of health insurance and have the financial capabilities to support risk associated with plans.

3) Create a market place via the Internet and phone-in service where qualified insurance companies can sell their insurance plans at their prices.

4) All consumers can shop for health insurance plans and purchase the plan they want and can afford. This shopping effort will be a free-market driver that will keep costs at reasonable levels.

5) If consumers can't afford any plan, the lowest cost High-Deductible Plan will be provided at no cost and this premium cost will be paid for by Trial Town. They will need to provide proof of income and assets each year to qualify for this option.

6) Age will be a factor that will be allowed for insurance companies to discriminate on the price of plans. Pre-existing conditions won't be allowed as a discriminatory selection criterion.

7) All private insurance offered by employers will be discontinued. Employers currently offering plans can offer a stipend to their employees to purchase plans but can't purchase plans on behalf of their employees any longer."

Sammy then presented a table that showed the projected costs of the Health Marketplace Plan.

Government Health Marketplace (Plan)

Pop Category	P Ins	Poor	Elderly	Uninsured	
Raw Cost ($000)	**$ 541,837**	**$ 54,000**	**$ 100,699**	**$ 119,420**	
Insurance $	$ 54,184			$ 11,942	Government
Profit $	$ 54,184	$ (540)	$ (1,007)	$ 11,942	$ 347,233
Govt OH $	$ 16,255	$ 10,800	$ 20,140	$ 3,583	Private
Ind Care $	$ -				$ 650,205
TOTAL Cost ($000	**$ 666,460**	**$ 64,260**	**$ 119,832**	**$ 146,886**	**$ 997,438**

Sammy said, "I believe if we implement this plan, overall healthcare costs will drop close to pre- Government Plan levels."

"I just don't get it. Why will this plan result in a lower overall cost than the plan we've already tried?"

Sammy smiled. "It's all about leveraging free-market pressures to keep costs in line. Insurance companies now need to sell policies to individuals instead of large companies that get special deals. They will need to keep costs low or they will not be successful selling plans to the consumer market place. Insurance companies will need to work with healthcare professionals to keep costs at reasonable levels or healthcare professionals will not get business from insurance companies. The government's role in this entire process is:

- setting up definitions of care;
- establishing laws requiring all to participate in the program; and
- paying for those who genuinely cannot afford to pay for insurance."

I challenged Sammy. "But you're saying that folks who cannot afford insurance will be provided with a high-deductible plan. If these folks can't afford health insurance, how can they afford to pay for healthcare up to these high-deductible levels?"

"I did consider that fact, but I didn't feel government-provided healthcare plans should be the cream of the crop. Instead, I felt that the subsidized plans should cover a minimum that will prevent someone from going bankrupt if they can't afford insurance. Most uninsured people currently have some ability to pay for minor healthcare. They can't afford ongoing premiums and are wiped out if they have a health incident that's catastrophic."

I offered another objection to Sammy's plan. "Why do employers have to kick off all employees from their plans? I'm guessing you'll be upsetting some people who are getting a great health insurance deal from their employers."

"With some research we found that employers are paying about one third the costs of individuals who purchase healthcare coverage in the private market. This is because large employers have such large pools of people and can negotiate sweetheart deals for their employees. This negotiating power skews the marketplace and will continue to be a problem if allowed to continue in the Health Marketplace program."

"Won't insurance companies charge more if they don't have such large blocks of people in their risk pool?"

"This was an initial concern. However, car insurance is sold to individuals without employers. Insurance companies will have to build up a large pool of individuals through a free-market rather than catering to large employers."

"I have to admit your plan does make sense. However, so have all the other plans. We think that we can afford the plan, but then we are shocked with the results once the plans are implemented."

After my meeting with Sammy, I once again presented the plan to my city council. I was a little surprised to get a unanimous response to go ahead. When I questioned two of the council members who had previously voted no, they responded that the free-market drivers in Sammy's plan were quite attractive and they felt those drivers would keep the plan costs in line.

So, there I was, sitting in my office one year after we had implemented Sammy's Health Marketplace Plan when Sammy poked his head in my office. Once again, he invited me into the city hall conference room.

I expected to get another disappointing shock. Just as I had in previous visits to the conference room. He once again had his chart up on the projector screen.

Government Health Marketplace (Plan)

Pop Category	P Ins	Poor	Elderly	Uninsured	
Raw Cost ($000)	**$ 541,837**	**$ 54,000**	**$ 100,699**	**$ 119,420**	
Insurance $	$ 54,184			$ 11,942	Government
Profit $	$ 54,184	$ (540)	$ (1,007)	$ 11,942	$ 347,233
Govt OH $	$ 16,255	$ 10,800	$ 20,140	$ 3,583	Private
Ind Care $	$ -				$ 650,205
TOTAL Cost ($000	**$ 666,460**	**$ 64,260**	**$ 119,832**	**$ 146,886**	**$ 997,438**

Government Health Marketplace (Actual)

Pop Category	P Ins	Poor	Elderly	Uninsured	
Raw Cost ($000)	**$ 565,721**	**$ 54,000**	**$ 100,699**	**$ 95,536**	
Insurance $	$ 50,915			$ 9,554	Government
Profit $	$ 50,915	$ (540)	$ (1,007)	$ 8,598	$ 288,261
Govt OH $	$ 4,877	$ 5,400	$ 10,070	$ 1,075	Private
Ind Care $	$ -				$ 667,551
TOTAL Cost ($000	**$ 672,428**	**$ 58,860**	**$ 109,762**	**$ 114,762**	**$ 955,812**

Sammy was smiling from ear to ear. "Boss, I think you'll like the charts this time around."

As I quickly looked at the bottom line of healthcare costs of $956 million versus the $997 million per year that had been anticipated, I had to express my delight. "Sammy, it looks like you've done it. Overall costs are lower than what we had even anticipated this time last year. What's going on?"

Sammy laughed. "Boss, I told you that the free-market drivers of my plan would naturally drive down costs. Once insurance companies and healthcare professionals lost their captive large employer customers, they had to earn individual consumer's business. This resulted in lower profit margins and lower costs to ensure they would capture healthcare consumers."

I had to ask. "Sammy you show a decrease in cost for Uninsured. Why would these costs go lower than projected? I thought these were folks who could not afford insurance in the first place."

"After we implemented our 'income verification' system to verify low income level qualification, many of the uninsured could actually afford their own health insurance and so Trial Town doesn't have to pay for these folks."

"Sammy, it sure seems like this was a great first year. Is this kind of financial performance going to be successful over the long-term?"

"Mayor, I believe that this system will get better over time and reduce ongoing increases in healthcare costs as healthcare professionals and insurance companies try to win consumers."

I was certainly happy about the news, but felt I needed to play devil's advocate. "Okay, with these low prices and the marketplace saturated with all Trial Town's citizens, I'll bet there are long waiting lines for health care."

"It's interesting how the long lines disappeared when healthcare professionals were concerned about losing prospective consumers. This forced healthcare professionals and insurance providers to become more efficient without reducing quality. This is exactly the way that other free-markets in our community work. If a product costs too much or is of poor quality, consumers will not buy it. This same dynamic had been missing in healthcare for quite some time and is now responsible for driving health care costs down and healthcare quality up."

I had to respond to Sammy's free-market belief. "Sammy, I simply don't believe you. We have a fixed number of people. These people need healthcare. The demand for this service is the same as before. We have no more health professionals than we had before. Why wouldn't lines still be long?"

Sammy smiled. "I'll give you one example of what I'm talking about. One insurance company, Healthwise Inc., came up with an ingenious idea to reduce health procedure costs. They offered a discount on insurance premiums to consumers who would get at least three prices for each medical procedure they needed. This put competitive pressure on hospitals and doctors to offer lower cost procedures and still provide quality service."

I then smiled. "Sammy, you're now proving my point. If the costs of these procedures drop, demand will go up, creating long lines. You were the one who lectured me on the law of supply and demand in our meeting a year ago. Why are there no long lines?"

Sammy laughed as he responded. "Mayor, many consumers have opted to purchase higher deductible plans to save their own money on premiums. This means that many healthcare consumers are not using the hospitals, doctors and prescription services unless they absolutely have to use this care."

"I still don't understand. Are you saying that people were using healthcare when they didn't actually need care?"

"Yes, Mayor. That's exactly what I'm saying. Most of the folks that had free healthcare from the government or from employers were very eager to visit the doctor for anything. However, when the consumer understood that they could save their own money by using a high-deductible system and see the doctor less, that's what they did."

"What if folks don't see the doctor and have a bigger problem downstream? Won't this end up costing our healthcare system even more?"

Sammy smiled again. "Some insurance companies have now started offering discounts on premiums to cover this very issue. If consumers enroll in a Wellness Program that includes pre-screening for health issues, these consumers will get a discount on their premiums. You see, Mayor, these insurance companies are quite creative when they can quickly connect price to actions. This kind of connection never existed in our previous Government Care plan or in the original insurance system."

"Pre-screening won't reduce healthcare issues. In fact, I think this process could actually drive more folks to seek more expensive medical care."

"The Wellness Programs don't just include pre-screening. There are exercise and diet recommendations that result from these pre-screens that will prevent many problems like diabetes, obesity, and heart disease. Besides cancer, these three diseases are the most costly healthcare concerns in our community."

"I get it. I get it. Do you have anything more to share about our Health Marketplace Plan?"

"Boss, the other benefit that I really hadn't anticipated was the employers who were so happy to get rid of healthcare coverage as one of their benefits."

"I'll bet they were. This is one less cost that they'll have to pay, allowing them to make even more profits."

"Mayor, most employers still paid employees a stipend no lower than their health insurance subsidy was in the past. So they didn't directly save any money on health insurance per se."

"So why were these employers so happy about the Health Marketplace Plan?"

"Employers could reduce the administrative staff in charge of negotiating healthcare plans on an annual basis. They could also focus on their core business instead of always worrying about the variable and escalating costs of healthcare as a cost of doing business."

"I knew it. Now unemployment will probably go back up due to these layoffs of administrative workers."

"Actually, Mayor, Trial Town has hired many of these benefits administrators to set up the insurance marketplace to allow folks to shop for insurance policies. They have also helped with setting up the different insurance offerings."

I had to offer another obvious objection. "What about forcing all citizens of Trial Town to purchase health insurance? Isn't this a violation of their liberty?"

Sammy was a little more serious with this response. "Yes, Mayor, this is a violation of personal liberty. Some citizens have refused to purchase any of the health insurance packages offered."

"So what do you plan to do about that? After all, we can't tread on people's individual liberties, can we?"

"You're right, Mayor. We should not force folks to purchase anything."

I smiled. "There you have it, Sammy; a hole in your Health Marketplace Plan."

Sammy was deep in thought and then responded, "I believe that we should allow citizens to not purchase health insurance at all. This should be their right. If these folks have a healthcare problem, they'll need to pay for the required healthcare on their own."

"Won't this mess up the risk pool that insurance companies rely on to keep insurance premiums low?"

"Currently, 2,000 citizens out of our 100,000 citizens in Trial Town have refused to purchase health insurance. Out of these 2,000, 1,800 of them are young and in good health so this is a reduction in a pool of folks who could help reduce the overall healthcare risk."

"What are we supposed to do? Should we throw these citizens in jail? Should we charge them a penalty of some sort?"

Sammy smiled. "Mayor, Trial Town was founded on the basis of 'liberty for all.' Neither of those penalties is really necessary."

"What do you mean? You said that we need the young folks to purchase health insurance to balance out the risk in our healthcare system."

"I didn't say that, Mayor. Since insurance companies are allowed to discriminate based on age, older folks pay higher premiums. The free market has already built in the higher risk of older participants."

I couldn't let Sammy's assertion stand. "What about that uninsured person who comes into the emergency room with a life-threatening illness that must be treated by medical professionals?"

"First of all, this individual would have been deemed to have the financial resources to afford insurance or they would be on the government-subsidized system. In this situation, this person would have to come up with the financial resources to pay for their medical care. This could mean borrowing money or selling their assets. Along with liberty comes personal responsibility."

"Sammy, I want to thank you for coming up with such a brilliant plan that worked so well. Can you present the results of the Health Marketplace Plan to our city council in our meeting next week?"

"I would be glad to, Mayor."

I was a little embarrassed that Sammy was able to come up with such a successful plan when my previous plans were complete flops. I think I need to give this guy a raise.

Sammy presented his great news to our city council in our next city council meeting and they were elated. Finally a government program that we tried where we did not need to hit the reset button. Trial Town also voted to rescind the mandatory requirement originally put in our Health Marketplace Plan to preserve individual liberty. We still had some left over debt from two years of the failed Government Care plan. I had a feeling that Sammy's Health Marketplace Plan would erase a lot of this debt with higher corporate income taxes from improved corporate profits. I also believed that this program would ultimately lower health care costs as insurance providers continued to be innovative at lowering their costs to attract consumers.

Real World Examples

President Obama and the US Congress passed a quite extensive and complex law called the Affordable Care Act, otherwise known as Obama Care. Although this program has not yet been implemented in full, it is already showing the same negative signs of the original Government Care plan enacted by Trial Town. The Affordable Care Act was intended to mandate coverage that is more comprehensive than traditional plans. This by itself forces insurance companies to cancel non-compliant policies, forcing participants to enter the government marketplace system. Employers have been shifting full-time employees to part-time status to avoid paying for the mandatory healthcare coverage on full-time employees. This means that many employed Americans are forced to purchase their own insurance in the federal government marketplace.

In most cases, insurance premium prices being advertised on the Affordable Care Act web site (HealthCare.gov) are higher than health insurance coverage offered through employers. Many consumers will opt to simply not participate in purchasing insurance and pay the tax penalty that is levied as part of the Affordable Care Act. If these non-participants have some health event, they will simply buy into the marketplace system and then see a doctor, as there are no pre-existing condition restrictions. This will drive up health insurance and healthcare costs for the rest of those trying to participate in employer programs, Medicare, or Medicaid.

If the US utilized a Sammy-like system, I believe that the free-market drivers will work very similar to our hypothetical situation with Trial Town and drive down healthcare costs. A key to this working in the case of the United States is that health plans will need to be leaner than the current minimum requirements of the Affordable Care Act. There may need to be more plan options than what we outlined in the Trial Town case. For instance, plans that do not include maternity care; exclude birth control pills; do not pay for abortions or sex change operations and many other items that are not considered covered items in most private healthcare plans currently. These fully loaded plans can certainly be available but they should not establish the minimum plan coverage. This one factor has dramatically driven up the cost of health insurance premiums in the current Obama Care system.

Even though it seems like Trial Town figured out a system that could drive healthcare costs down and provide some safety net for those who cannot afford health insurance, the lowest cost system would have been paying for indigent care and having an open-market place for health care procedures. This would not have necessarily solved any of the situations that Mary described at the beginning of this story but it still would provide a safety net for those who could not afford needed healthcare. Unfortunately, people could still be wiped out financially if they do not have coverage.

I know that this system was touted as a success by Sammy and Arthur at the end of the story. However, this community almost exchanged a piece of liberty for a sense of financial security. In our current system, as in the originally proposed Health Marketplace Plan, all citizens are forced to purchase health insurance. This is a clear violation of our basic liberty. It is somewhat analogous to having to purchase car insurance in many states in order to utilize the privilege to drive a car. Even in these instances, many drivers do not purchase car insurance and thus we have to have Uninsured Motorist insurance. The same problem will occur with health insurance. Many will simply refuse to make the mandatory purchase. In the current Affordable Care Act, there is a tax penalty levied on people refusing to purchase health insurance, which is less than annual health care premiums. I am guessing many will refuse to purchase health insurance and refuse to pay the penalty and will then be put in jail. This is not the type of free society that promotes liberty and self-reliance. Instead, it promotes government dependency and rule by force.

The system that existed in Trial Town prior to any government intervention was probably a workable system. The Health Marketplace idea could have been implemented completely separately as a private sector innovation with no cost to tax payers. Indigent care would still cover those who have no means to pay for services. Unfortunately, a person's wealth can be wiped out with a single severe health incident. This has been the choice we humans have had since the beginning of time. Is our wealth a reasonable exchange for our health? That is not an unfair or inhumane decision. It is simply part of life. When the question is turned around in a national healthcare environment: Is someone else's wealth more important than my health? The answer will always be 'no' and healthcare costs will increase without limit.□

7 GREENING TRIAL TOWN

"In reality, studies show that investments to spur renewable energy and boosts in energy efficiency generate far more jobs than oil and coal."
— Jeff Goodell

It was a crisp fall day and I decided I would take a drive to the mountains to see the changing fall colors. I pulled into my local gas station and noticed that the price of gasoline had risen from $1.80 to $1.99 per gallon. This certainly caught my attention, but I felt it was still worth it to go see the new fall colors. I then noticed as I drove to the mountains, that several other people had the same idea as I did, and traffic was heavy. I also could not help but notice that most drivers had only one person in the car.

I thought, "We seem to use a lot of fuel and I'm concerned that we have limited supplies. Why is gasoline so expensive? Why do we insist on driving with a single driver to simply see fall colors changing? Why can't we develop alternatives to gasoline, coal and diesel to prevent excessive pollution and have a more sustainable energy source?"

After I returned from my joy ride, I felt I needed to have this clean energy discussion with my friend Chuck Stanfield, the owner of a local solar energy company.

I set up my meeting with Chuck and was pleased that he was available to meet on Tuesday morning at the coffee shop.

"Hi, Mayor," Chuck said, welcoming me to the coffee shop.

"Hi, Chuck." We both made our coffee orders and sat down near the coffee shop window. "I'm glad that you could meet with me today, Chuck."

"I'm always glad to meet with you, Arthur. What's on your mind?"

"This last weekend, I took a joy ride to see the fall colors in the mountains. As I started on my ride, I noticed that gasoline prices seem to continue to rise. I noticed several people driving up to the mountains with only one passenger in their car. It bothers me that we continue to use a limited fuel source that's escalating in price and is causing damage to our environment."

"Arthur, you're preaching to the choir! I'm with you. That's why I started my solar energy company."

"Chuck, I want to ask you. Given the situation of escalating fuel prices, and the imminent pollution problems, I would guess that your business is doing quite well. After all, you're getting folks off fossil fuels and into renewable solar energy products."

"Actually, Arthur, business has been slow. We've completed free estimates for many merchants, home owners, and many local government stakeholders but we're not getting many sales at all."

"Wow, I'm so surprised. Why are people not buying your product? You're giving them free energy from the sun. How could they say no?"

Chuck hung his head. "Well, it isn't quite that simple. The solar energy panels that I install are relatively new technology and they are quite expensive. Even though they can generate free energy once installed, they cost so much money that it'll take many prospective buyers 40 years to recover their initial investment. Once they understand this financial truth, they quickly say no."

I was astonished. "Those simple panels are that expensive? They don't look like much. I thought they would be relatively cheap."

"I understand. When I got into this business, I was a little surprised myself. The solar manufacturers tell me that the cost is high because their sales volume is low. If we were able to sell more, the price should come down as manufacturers can make more solar panels."

We discussed a lot more business facts. I was convinced that Trial Town could do something to help. Why can't we get this great technology out there and help Chuck in his business?

"Chuck," I offered, "do you think it would help if Trial Town pays half the cost of the solar installations to get the return on investment to 20 years?"

Chuck smiled, "Arthur that would be a great idea. Can you afford to do something like this in Trial Town's budget?"

"We have been getting a lot of pressure from many in our community who are equally concerned about our dependence on fossil fuel. I think that the public will be pleased that we are taking active steps to promote this clean fuel source."

After my meeting with Chuck Stanfield, I met with our city council and explained my environmental concerns and the idea of incentivizing folks to invest in energy conservation and energy efficiency. The city council voted 4-2 to pass a law that allowed for a one-time collection of $500 from each person in Trial Town to raise a total of $50 million to incentivize solar energy projects.

I was very excited about this project and believed that Trial Town could greatly reduce its dependency on fossil fuels, improve our environment and become a much more financially viable community.

I shared the news with Chuck, and he quickly started printing up new marketing information to promote the new government programs to subsidize solar panel installations. Chuck was also quite creative at working on financing solutions for prospective clients so that they would not have to pay anything as long as the Trial Town subsidy was in place. Chuck did this by financing his installations for 20 years. The annual payments equaled the cost savings produced by his solar panels. This allowed people to purchase solar energy systems free of charge.

I could tell that the program was a success as we had over 800 applications for solar panel subsidies. All of the applications were approved and many projects were implemented within the first year of the program. I noticed solar panels on houses, merchant buildings and several government buildings. I was quite happy with myself and felt we had genuinely done a lot of good in our community. Not only did we reduce our consumption of fossil fuel, we probably generated a lot of tax revenue from the boost to our local economy.

As I was sitting in my office patting myself on the back for my successful solar energy program, my phone rang.

I answered, "Mayor Wallaby."

I heard an excited voice on the other end of the line. "Hey, Mayor, it's me, Chuck."

"Hi, Chuck. I'll bet you are doing gangbusters with the solar energy incentive program."

"Mayor, we've had one of our best years ever. We fared well as we got a jump on most of the marketing. However, three other companies from Capital City heard about the new incentive program and they also ramped up their sales efforts in Trial Town."

"I suppose that was bound to happen. But I bet you made out pretty well, didn't you?"

"Like I said, Arthur," Chuck responded, "this was by far our most successful year. I hired an additional ten installers, and we had $15 million in revenue this year with an additional $15 million planned for next year."

I puffed my chest out a little. "So it sounds like the program was a great success. I'm glad to hear things went well for you."

Chuck sounded a little down when he responded. "Mayor, the reason for my call is that I spoke with Sammy Penbrook regarding my last solar energy rebate application and Sammy indicated to me that Trial Town was out of funds and unable to continue to subsidize solar energy projects."

"Chuck, our solar energy subsidy program was intended to jump start the market. I really don't think we can get additional funds to continue to fund more projects. Two of the city council members were against this program because we are basically charging all tax payers $500 to fund projects that most of those folks won't benefit from personally."

Chuck now sounded a little stressed. "Arthur, I don't think you understand the situation. If these subsidies stop, our business will go down sharply after we complete the $15 million worth of installations we have planned for this coming year."

"Chuck, I don't understand. Didn't the price of the panels drop with the large amount of orders you were able to provide?"

"Prices did drop slightly but not really enough to make up for the subsidy."

"Say, Chuck, I'll try to go back to the city council and see if they'd be willing to fund another round of subsidies at a lower rate of $400 per person in Trial Town. Maybe they will see that we are going in the right direction and vote in favor."

"Sounds good, Mayor. Thanks for your help."

I did what I promised Chuck but I was a little shocked at the negative reaction by our city council. When I put forward the proposal to raise another round of funds to fund more solar projects, the city council voted 4-2 against the move. What a bad city council meeting. I felt I was completely unprepared for it. I did present the financial benefits experienced by Chuck's company, but was not very articulate at communicating any other benefits that we were getting from the solar energy program. What about the jobs that had been added as a result of our investment? What about the tax revenues that were made as a result of all of the business that was generated in such a short time? What about the added productivity that was generated as a result of businesses, governments and home owners not having to pay high utility bills? I felt I needed to meet again with Chuck to better prepare to present these benefits to the city council.

Chuck and I met again at our coffee shop. After we sat down with our coffees in hand, I started the conversation. "Chuck, I have some disappointing news. The city council voted against my proposal to continue the Trial Town subsidies for solar energy."

"That's disappointing news."

"Chuck, I think I may still be able to get the plan to continue if I can better articulate many of the benefits of the program."

Chuck showed a little excitement. "How can I help?"

"Chuck, I need you to fill in some information for me to better sell this idea to the city council."

"Ask away!"

"Can you tell me what net annual financial benefit your customers are seeing as a result of your solar energy installations?"

"Well, they are actually not seeing any net financial benefit right away. All of the cost savings are used to pay for the installation of the solar panels for 20 years."

"Okay… so that angle won't work. What about the amount of money that you made this past year? How much will you pay in income taxes for that added income?"

Chuck smiled. "We did well this past year, making a net profit of $1.5 million, which means that we'll pay 15% of this in Trial Town income taxes for a total benefit to the city of additional $225,000 tax revenue. I believe next year will be equally profitable, adding another $225,000 in tax revenues."

"Now we're getting somewhere. How much tax revenue will come back to Trial Town as a result of all of the solar energy projects we helped fund with our program?"

"Well, I was the only Trial Town solar energy company making installations as part of this program. I'm assuming the Capital City companies that completed installations will benefit Capital City's tax revenue but not help Trial Town's tax revenue at all."

"I never thought about outsider companies taking advantage of this program. I guess that's the way it goes. What about your installers? They make a salary and have to pay 15% income tax. How much in tax revenues do you think resulted from employing these folks?"

"I had to add ten installers at $35,000 per person, so I'd guess that this would add an additional $52,500 per year to Trial Town taxes at a 15% income tax rate."

"Okay… in financial benefits, I'm seeing a total of $555,000 in net financial benefits to Trial Town over two years. Am I missing something?"

"Well, we're also reducing fossil fuel energy consumption."

"Great point! About how much of a dent did we make in reducing our fossil fuel consumption?"

Chuck said, "All of the solar energy projects will result in a reduction of

36 million kilowatt-hours in energy consumption. This is about 0.5% of our community's electricity consumption. This amounts to a reduction of $2.7 million in utility costs and a reduction of burning 19,000 tons of polluting coal."

"Those seem to be some great statistics. I think I have what I need for my next city council meeting."

After our meeting I was somewhat disappointed by the anemic statistics of the solar energy program. I was impressed with the fact that we had made some headway but I started anticipating the hard questions that would be asked by my city council. I then questioned how prepared I was to sell a renewal of this program. I decided to set up a meeting with Sammy Penbrook, our tax assessor. He was a numbers wiz and could help me present these statistics in the best light.

I met Sammy in our city hall conference room after I had given him all of the statistics that Chuck had given me. I started the meeting. "Sammy, I think you can help me sell a renewal of our solar energy incentive program to the city council."

Sammy paused and then responded, "I did some research after you invited me to this meeting. I'm not sure I have the best news for you about the solar energy program."

At that point, he showed a table up on the projector screen.

Tax Revenue Category	Amount	
Solar Energy Tax Revenues (2-yrs)	$	555,000
Utility Tax Lost Revenues (20-yrs)	$	(1,205,357)
Trial Town Net Benefit	**$**	**(650,357)**

"Mayor, it's true that Trial Town will gain revenue from added jobs and income taxes from the initial project installations. As you may know, the utility company also pays taxes to Trial Town. The solar installations will result in a reduction of revenue by the utilities. Their reductions in revenues will result in a reduction in profit at the utility company and thus a reduction in Trial Town tax revenues."

"But Sammy, you have evaluated the positive revenues over 2 years but the negative revenues over 20 years. That doesn't seem to be a fair comparison to support our solar energy incentive program."

"Mayor, the reduction in energy consumption lasts for at least 20 years while the positive revenue will only last as long as Trial Town continues to incentivize solar energy projects. According to you, Chuck's company can't continue solar projects after Trial Town subsidies end. So this positive revenue will stop at the end of 2 years."

I hung my head. "So let me get this straight. We raised $50 million from our community to invest in solar energy projects, which eventually ended up costing our city and additional $650,000 over the life of this project? And we only reduced energy consumption in our community by 0.5%?"

"You are close to right. We actually reduced electricity consumption by 0.5%. We use a substantial amount of heating fuel and gasoline for our cars, so the actual impact to reducing fossil fuel energy is closer to 0.1%."

"Thanks for making the situation sound even worse."

"Sorry boss, just trying to give you the facts."

"Sammy, I really appreciate the work you've done here. I'm not hearing what I want but it's good to know the truth. Thank you."

"Sure thing boss. Let me know if you need anything further."

After our meeting, I was heartbroken. There was simply no way that I could go back in front of the city council to ask for a second round of this financing, knowing that we were taking funds from our community that were really not providing much of a benefit to those people either directly or indirectly.

I met again with Chuck to give him the bad news. Chuck was certainly disappointed but even he understood why I could not get the city council to approve a second round of incentives.

A year later, as I was sitting in my office, I heard a knock on my door. "Come in."

The door opened and it was Chuck. "Hi, Mayor. Do you have some time to talk?"

"Sure, Chuck," I responded. "How are things going?"

"Not so good, Mayor," Chuck responded, a frown on his face.

"I suppose you had to downsize after our incentive programs went away. That's certainly a hard thing to go through," I said.

"Arthur, downsizing would have been better than closing my doors."

I was shocked. "What? You went out of business. Why?"

"Things were going really good with the incentive program. When the incentives stopped, many prospective customers were insistent that Trial Town would reinstitute an incentive program at some future date and so they insisted on waiting."

I interrupted. "Are you saying that our initial program actually created expectations that eventually damaged your business?"

"The waiting delayed revenues. Eventually I couldn't pay bills without revenue from new installations. At first, I laid off installers, but I simply couldn't make any new sales. So I had to close the doors."

"Chuck, I'm so sorry. I thought that the Trial Town solar energy program would give you the boost you needed. Instead you're out of business."

Chuck gave an awkward smile. "I'm okay. I did keep some of the cash that I made early in the program and I plan to start a new business. I stopped by just to let you know how things are going."

"I'm sorry to hear about your business closing. Please let me know if I can do anything to help you in the future."

"Arthur, I do appreciate all that you did. I guess it's just not the right time for solar energy projects."

After this final meeting with Chuck, I was more educated about how energy incentive programs work and I don't think I will ever propose this kind of plan again. In the end, we really did not save much energy. The incentives cost our community in its initial investment then it cost even more in lost tax revenues from utility companies. On top of all of these negative results, we disrupted a local businessman's business even though we tried to help. I cannot see a "win" in any of this.

Real World Examples

Several federal, state and local governments and utilities have invested billions of dollars in utility rebate and incentive programs since the 1970s. In the case of utility companies, incentive funds are raised from utility ratepayers to pay for rebates offered for energy efficient products and services. In the case of government rebates, they have come in the form of tax credits and direct project investments in the form of grants. In many cases, governments will offer both tax credits and grants, which create a double cost to these government entities.

A few of the largest government investment programs happened in the late 1970s with the advent of the OPEC oil embargo; and most recently a massive stimulus program in 2009 designed to improve recessional economic conditions by putting people to work. The term "Green Jobs" was coined in the 2000s with the promise of improved employment from this new green economy. In some cases, the federal government directly subsidized private solar companies that ultimately went bankrupt after a substantial amount of tax funds were lost in these ventures.

Green technologies, solar energy, energy efficiency projects and renewable energy generation projects are certainly meritorious projects deserving the same fair evaluation as any other projects. The reality is that government subsidies for green projects tend to be "money for nothing" and result in disrupting a free-market industry rather than helping the industry. Just like the story in Trial Town, many companies that were chasing government subsidies and utility rebates in 2009 to 2010 were downsizing and going out of business in 2011 when the market could not continue without government subsidies that had essentially gone away. In many cases, building owners that rushed into the energy efficiency business with the promise of government subsidies in this brief time period diminished the market that could have been gained in the normal course of business with energy efficiency companies that were already present and thriving prior to the injection of government subsidies.

The other argument commonly heard to promote energy efficiency and renewable energy projects include an environmental appeal to reduce global warming, reduce general pollution or simply make our earth cleaner. These desires are certainly legitimate and admirable. Unfortunately, promised environmental benefits are often exaggerated.

You also may have noted in the Trial Town story that all people had to pay $500 when the city raised revenue to support the solar energy program. This means that the poor and rich tend to pay equally for energy conservation incentive programs. However, most of the beneficiaries of these incentive programs are the wealthy or government institutions, since they are more able to afford costly energy efficiency projects with or without government subsidies. This effectively is a tax on the poor since they have to pay utility rate increases or government taxes, but do not benefit from the actual rebates and government tax incentives given to the wealthy.

8 Trial Town goes to War

"Over grown military establishments are under any form of government inauspicious to liberty, and are to be regarded as particularly hostile to republican liberty."
— George Washington

Trial Town had always funded a robust military that was perfectly capable of protecting Trial Town. Trial Town invests $240 million per year in a military comprised of 2,400 troops who are staffed to protect Trial Town. In some cases, Trial Town's military augments with other neighboring towns to help with other military protection needed in foreign countries.

In Trial Town's world, there are always requests for Trial Town's military to help win a war in some far off land. The most recent request was quite compelling. Trial Town gets most of its oil from Oil Shores, a faraway land that is rich with crude oil reserves. Capital City also gets most of its oil from this same location. Both Capital City and Trial Town have their own refineries to produce gasoline but they need oil from Oil Shores in order to supply the fuel necessary for Capital City and Trial Town's citizens.

When I picked up today's newspaper, I was shocked to read that Oil

Shores was under threat of attack by Sand Shores, its neighbor. Sand Shores also has oil reserves. Unfortunately, Sand Shores has been reluctant to sell oil to either Capital City or Trial Town. I immediately called up the mayor of Capital City, Don Westland.

"Hi, Don, this is Arthur Wallaby in Trial Town."

"Hi Arthur", Don responded. "What can I do for you?"

"Did you see the headlines in the paper today regarding Oil Shores?" I asked.

"I haven't had a chance to read the paper. Can you enlighten me?"

"It looks like Sand Shores may be a threat to Oil Shores. I think we ought to mobilize our military to protect oil interests in this region. You know that we both rely on Oil Shores for our oil and energy needs. If this oil is cut off or costs us twice as much with Sand Shores, this can negatively impact us both."

Don said, "Are you kidding? I wasn't aware of this problem. I agree that we ought to collectively station troops in this region."

We both met with our city councils and got approval to move our troops to Oil Shores to protect our oil interests.

Three months later, we both realized that we were in over our head. It turned out that after moving troops over to protect Oil Shores, the cost to station these troops abroad would cost us more than what was in our military budget. We both decided it was worthwhile borrowing funds for this temporary situation, as it should go away in the next few years. We thought that we could somehow reduce other government expenses and pay off this debt. Trial Town's added share of the expense of stationing troops in Oil Shore would be $100 million per year until hostilities ended in the region.

Six months later, we were glad that we had stationed troops in Oil Shores. Sand Shores did attack in an attempt to take over Oil Shore's valuable oil reserves. Capital City and Trial Town had to add to its debt in order to afford the additional equipment and ammunition required during this fighting phase. Trial Town's share of this increased cost was an additional $100 million per year.

While our military was busy fighting in Oil Shores, I learned that another skirmish was brewing in Landingham. Landingham supplied us with diamonds. If we lost our relationship with the leaders of Landingham, we would certainly lose the low-cost diamonds that we needed for our jewelry industry. I went to the city council with my case and they agreed that we needed to send additional troops to defend the diamond mines in Landingham. This required an additional $150 million per year.

Two years later, because of our involvement in both the Landingham and Oil Shores' conflicts, we were spending $400 million per year over our peacetime military budget. Even with these investments, there were terrorist bombings of the oil wells in Oil Shores and similar bombings in the Landingham diamond mines. In addition to our budget cost overruns, our military personnel were losing their lives in these wars. In total, Capital City and Trial Town lost 800 troops over the over two years.

I was getting a lot of flak from local citizens about the cost in lives and in money from both of these wars. In fact, many people were so upset about our involvement; they were threatening to fire me.

After three years of having troops stationed in Landingham and Oil Shores, we then were attacked in our local community. Just before we were to begin wheat-harvesting season, a group of foreign terrorists set our wheat fields on fire and destroyed our entire wheat crop for the coming year.

At this point, I got approval from our city council to increase our military expenditures by an additional $100 million per year to protect our local factories, government facilities and agricultural lands.

At the end of three years, we were fighting three separate military campaigns. We were managing to keep our head above water but our debt was climbing yearly and I was not fully convinced the investment in our military effort was making much of a difference.

Sammy Penbrook poked his head in my office. "Say boss, I'd like to talk to you about some money problems we're having."

"Sure Sammy! Come on in!"

Sammy put another one of his tables of numbers on my desk. The table showed the total amount that we had spent in addition to our current military budget to support all of the military campaigns that we had been waging over the past five years.

Military Campaign	**Added Annual Cost**	**Duration (Yrs)**	**Total Debt**
Oil Shores - Troops	$ 100,000,000	5	$ 500,000,000
Oil Shores - Fighting	$ 150,000,000	4.5	$ 675,000,000
Landingham - Troops	$ 150,000,000	3	$ 450,000,000
Homeland Protection	$ 100,000,000	2	$ 200,000,000
TOTALS			**$ 1,825,000,000**

Sammy opened our conversation. "Boss, we've dug ourselves quite the financial hole. Over the past five years, we've accumulated $1.825 trillion in debt to support military action abroad and at home."

I quickly responded, "Sammy, you don't understand. It doesn't matter the cost. If we don't actively engage in these areas with our military, we risk our very existence. We have to spend whatever it takes to win these conflicts."

Sammy fired back, "Mayor, I don't think you understand the financial side of this equation. Trial Town doesn't have an unlimited amount of finances. Nor will our creditors loan us an unlimited amount of money if they don't believe that we can pay it back."

"Are you saying that we are at the limit of the amount that we can borrow?" I asked.

"We can get creative and sell war bonds to fund additional debt. We still can also increase debt from our current creditors. However, at most, I think we can last two more years in our current military conflicts. After that, we'll have quite a large debt to pay off. Even if we increased taxes as high as we can, it will take over 20 years to pay this debt off."

"Sammy, these are very important decisions that go beyond our budget. I need to think about it a little more, before I let you know what we're going to do."

"I understand that these decisions go beyond our budget. Unfortunately, if we spend any more, we'll have no option but to pull our military out of these campaigns and we'll be broke. At that point, we won't be able to afford any military campaign and our enemies will know it. This will leave us even more vulnerable to attacks. Once we have been financially weakened to a point that we can't defend ourselves, we'll be in real trouble."

I was now aware of the major hole that we had dug. Trial Town had leveraged its entire future to fight wars to protect a few streams of critical resources. We had also lost valuable lives and were treating many others who had been wounded fighting in these battles. Sammy was right; we could not afford to keep this kind of military presence around the world. By fighting in so many wars, we were weakening our ability to defend Trial Town.

The next day I met with the mayor of Capital City to let him know I would be proposing pulling our troops out of Oil Shores. He seemed relieved when I gave him the news. It seems he was getting similar pressure to pull Capital City troops back home.

I met with my city council and gave them the same news that Sammy had given me only a few days earlier. A few city council members pushed back.

Paul Fredrick spoke up. "Mayor, I understand these conflicts are costing us a lot of money but I believe these communities will be devastated if we pull out. I also believe that Trial Town's safety and economy will be negatively impacted if we pull out."

"Paul, I share your concern. I just don't think we can afford to fight these wars regardless of the outcome. I have already spoken with the mayor of Capital City and he's on board with pulling Capital City troops out of Oil Shores. I believe that we should pull troops out of all foreign conflicts and maintain our troop levels at pre-war levels to simply protect Trial Town."

Paul responded, "Arthur, I think that you're just plain chicken. If we stick this out another few years, we could claim victory and then worry about paying off our debt. As it is, you're going to quit and undo all the good that we've done in these regions."

"Paul, I certainly respect your opinion, but I disagree. I don't think we've helped any of these regions. I don't think they are any safer now than when we started fighting. In retrospect, I don't think we should've ever gotten involved in these wars in the first place. If we have to pay a little more for oil from Sand Shores instead of Oil Shores, I believe that's a lot less costly than the human and financial cost we are paying now. The same goes for diamond prices."

Paul reacted, "What about the threats we have faced here in Trial Town? Do you remember when terrorists burned our wheat fields? I suppose we can't afford to even defend our own wheat fields."

"Paul, I feel we wouldn't have been attacked by foreign terrorists in our community if we didn't insist on getting involved in foreign conflicts. I want to invest the military we have in our base budget to protect Trial Town. I believe it isn't in our best interest to protect those in other countries."

Paul was noticeably angry. "Okay. Well, you know how I'm going to vote. The rest of you can make up your minds whether you want to be a bunch of chicken-quitters or if you want to do the honorable thing and see these military conflicts to a positive conclusion."

The discussion went on late into the night. The city council voted 4-2 to end the current military conflicts that we were engaged in abroad.

I tried to be as diplomatic as possible with Oil Shores and Landingham about the fact that we would be pulling our troops out of their countries. I recommended to both leaders that they develop their own militia so they could defend their land without intervention from Trial Town or Capital City. Neither leader was happy at the news that we would be quitting the wars that we had participated in for the last five years.

Over the next two years, we pulled troops out of Oil Shores and Landingham. After we had pulled our troops out, Sand Shores did make another concerted attack on Oil Shores and there was a lot of bloodshed. Sand Shores was experienced in terrorist tactics while the Oil Shore militia had learned a few tricks after fighting with Trial Town and Capital City troops over the past several years. Several troops died on both sides of this conflict. After a year of fighting, Sand Shores and Oil Shores arrived at an agreement splitting the revenues on oil wells that Sand Shores believed belonged on their land. After all our worry, the price of oil didn't go up at all.

Meanwhile in Landingham, the diamond mines were taken over by a corrupt government comprised of many of the terrorists who were bombing the mines. Landingham government officials worked out some financial arrangement with the new rogue government. But the resulting government was corrupt. To be fair, I think the old government was not that much better.

We did pull our troops all back to Trial Town and downsized our military to pre-war levels. We experienced no more attacks in Trial Town. We kept our military and police force on high alert for quite some time just in case other terror activities were attempted on our home soil.

By the time we had downsized our military, our debt had reached $2 trillion. I was very glad to be able to hit the reset button to get rid of the debt that we had accumulated from these military campaigns. Unfortunately, I could not hit a reset button to bring back the 1,000 Trial Town lives that had been lost in these military campaigns. Nor could I hit the reset button on the 3,000 Trial Town citizens who had been wounded. Troops experiencing severe psychological problems broke my heart.

One of the saddest things to me personally, was the fact that we really accomplished little with the investment of treasure and life.

Real World Examples

Military conflicts have been a part of the United States since our founding. We were able to win our independence from a restrictive King of England in our Revolutionary War. We then engaged in another war with Great Britain in the War of 1812, the Civil War in 1862, then World War I in 1914, then World War II in 1941, the Korean War, the Vietnam War, the Gulf War, the Afghanistan War, and the Iraq Invasion. I have certainly overlooked several other conflicts that the United States has engaged in since its inception as a country. There could be a debate about the worthiness of all of these military engagements. The common denominator in them all is that they have cost our country a substantial amount of money and valuable lives on both sides of the conflict. Most of them have resulted in increasing our national debt. Up to the Vietnam War, we had been in a place where we could always pay this debt back with increases in taxes for a limited amount of time.

In our modern times, there are three areas of interest for U.S. military action: 1) Ukraine; 2) Iraq; and 3) Afghanistan.

Ukraine: Russia has made two large plays to take over eastern regions of the Ukraine. Although, the U.S. considers Ukraine and ally, the U.S. has been reluctant to support Ukraine's resistance against Russian rebels within their country.

Iraq: In December 2011, most U.S troops had been withdrawn from Iraq after removing Saddam Hussein from power and verifying there were no weapons of mass destruction or terrorist training camps. Ironically, in 2014, Iraq has been invaded by an Islamic Extremist group called ISIS (Islamic State in Iraq and Syria). The U.S. has provided air strikes to support the local Iraqi Army, but has resisted installing ground troops.

Afghanistan: The U.S. invaded Afghanistan shortly after the Al-Qaida attack on the U.S. in September 2001. After leaving Afghanistan, to fight in Iraq in 2003, the U.S. increased troop support in Afghanistan in recent years. Many troops were withdrawn from Afghanistan in 2014 and several hope to be completely out of Afghanistan by the end of 2016.

I believe that President Obama has done an excellent job of resisting political pressure to put more U.S. troops in these regions. Meanwhile, we have several military personnel returning to our country with severe cases of depression and post-traumatic-stress-disorder (PTSD); and missing limbs and other physical wounds. On top of this, our Veterans Administration is not treating our troops for injuries they have obtained while fighting in these wars.

It is certainly understandable to upsize the military and military spending to defend the United States. However, most military conflicts since World War II have not been fought to defend the United States. Recent conflicts have been an attempt to influence how other governments operate.

Just as with any government activity, military activity cannot exceed budget restrictions for any period without damaging our country financially and creating enemies in places that would not normally consider the U.S. to be an enemy.

9 JOB INSECURITY

"Should any political party attempt to abolish social security, unemployment insurance, and eliminate labor laws and farm programs, you would not hear of that party again in our political history."
— Dwight D. Eisenhower

We were doing great in Trial Town. Our economy was booming; unemployment rates were at an all-time low of 4%; and we had a relatively low income tax rate of 15% for all Trial Town citizens. Our retirement programs were fully funded, and there was plenty of cash to pay retirees. We had experienced several years of prosperity. In fact, things were going a bit too good. We started to develop a surplus cash balance in Trial Town's bank account. It was at about this time I decided to have lunch with James Pennyworth, the local paper mill owner.

I met James at the Pirate's Cove to have lunch.

"Hi Mayor," James said. "How are things going with you?"

"James, things could not be better with Trial Town. I think our town has found the secret recipe to a successful government. In fact, I'm considering writing a book on how to run a successful government. How are things going at the paper mill?"

"Not so good, Arthur," James responded. "We are doing well with our profits. Unfortunately, Capital City just cancelled a few large paper orders. I had to lay off 100 employees at the mill just last week."

"That's too bad. What are those folks going to do to support their families?"

"I don't know. We gave them a few months' severance pay. Hopefully, they will find jobs after that."

"James," I interjected, "what if Trial Town offered to pay these folks a portion of their salary for a short time. Just until they can find other work?"

"How can the city afford to pay these salaries with no additional money coming in?" James asked.

"We have a small surplus," I responded. "Plus, this should be a temporary expense and will be a good investment to support these folks until they find new jobs."

"That makes me feel much better about having to deliver the bad news to those people. Thanks for this program," James said.

"I'll need to get the city council's approval but I think they'll be on board."

When I presented the idea to the city council, they unanimously supported weekly payments for the folks who had been laid off. The program started out as a payment of 80% of the salary they had prior to being laid off. The program would last for three months to provide some financial support for families until displaced employees could find employment with another company. We called the program the Displaced Worker's Program.

We then did a community-wide advertising campaign to let everyone know about the program. I was a little surprised by how many folks responded, I suppose the number of enrollees approximately matched our rate of unemployment of 4%.

Sammy Penbrook ran the numbers and calculated a total monthly cost of over $8 million. If these folks found jobs in less than three months, this cost should drop over time.

Displaced Workers Program (Start)		
Total Workforce		54,000
Unemployment Rate		4.0%
Unemployed Workers		2,160
Avg Annual Salary	$	55,000
Monthly Admin Cost	$	145,000
Monthly Cost	$	8,065,000

I got several pats on the back from many workers who had been laid off.

When the program had been in force for about three months, I checked back in with Sammy to see how the Displaced Worker's Program was succeeding. By this point, many folks should have found jobs and be productive tax-paying members of society.

I asked Sammy to brief me on how our budget was progressing.

Sammy came into my office with his typical stack of papers. "Well, boss, the Displaced Worker's Program has some good results and some bad results."

"Come on, Sammy, you're always coming into my office or into the conference room and bursting my bubble on a perfectly good program. Let's have it."

Sammy showed me a simple table, similar to the table he showed me before except that this table had a few more rows.

Displaced Workers Program (3-mo)	
Total Workforce	54,000
Unemployment Rate	4.5%
Disqualified	2.0%
Net Unemployed	2.5%
Unemployed Workers	1,350
Avg Annual Salary	$ 55,000
Monthly Admin Cost	$ 145,000
Monthly Cost	$ 5,095,000

Sammy started his briefing. "The bad news is that our unemployment rate in Trial Town rose by 0.5% up to 4.5%, so we have more unemployed folks than we had six months ago. The good news is that several employees who were receiving Displaced Worker's benefits have been unemployed longer than three months and so we are no longer paying them the benefit."

I had to interrupt. "Sammy, having people unemployed longer than three months is not good news."

Sammy responded with a smirk. "Sorry Mayor. I guess I was thinking about the budget for the Displaced Worker's Program and not the people in this situation. Overall, the net cost of the program has dropped from over $8 million per month to just over $5 million per month. This is a $3 million per month savings to Trial Town."

After hearing the whole picture, I had to react. "Sammy, this doesn't seem like good news at all. The 2% of the work force that can't find jobs are hurting. I'm sure those people don't feel our budget surplus is good news. I think I've underestimated the unemployment problem in our community. We can help these folks out instead of kicking them off the program."

Sammy then responded with a note of disappointment. "Mayor, this will drive our monthly cost from $5 million a month to approximately $9 million a month."

Displaced Workers Program II (3-mo)		
Total Workforce		54,000
Unemployment Rate		4.5%
Disqualified		0.0%
Net Unemployed		4.5%
Unemployed Workers		2,430
Avg Annual Salary	$	55,000
Monthly Admin Cost	$	145,000
Monthly Cost	$	9,055,000

I responded with a little impatience of my own. "Sammy, you're a numbers guy. I understand that we need to have some budget discipline. However, sometimes human need is more important than saving a few bucks."

"It's ultimately up to the city council and you to decide. I'll simply report the financials. Just don't blame me when we have another budget crisis."

"Thanks for your work on getting me these facts, Sammy. I'll let you know what the city council decides."

I went to the city council and explained that I felt we may have underestimated the unemployment problem in our community and we needed to extend the duration of the Displaced Worker's benefits for six months instead of three months. Three months didn't seem to be enough time for many people to get a new job. The city council voted 4-2 to approve an extension of the Displaced Worker's Program. Sammy then showed me an update of the budget for the program.

As before, I had asked Sammy for an update in three months.

When three months had passed, Sammy met me in my office with his simple table to show me how the program was progressing.

Displaced Workers Program II (6-mo)		
Total Workforce		54,000
Unemployment Rate		6.0%
Disqualified		2.0%
Net Unemployed		4.0%
Unemployed Workers		2,160
Avg Annual Salary	$	55,000
Monthly Admin Cost	$	145,000
Monthly Cost	$	8,065,000

"Boss, the table looks very similar to the table at our last three month period. Unemployment rose to 6% from 4.5% and the Displaced Worker's Program budget went back down to our original monthly amount with the disqualified workers who have been unemployed for more than six months."

I was upset. "What in the world is going on here? It must be a hard employment environment out there. I'm going to try to get this program extended one more time. I hope that we'll be able to get out of this situation."

"Sammy, before I get back to the city council, what do you think is causing these unemployment numbers to rise?" I asked.

"I'm not sure. We do show the majority of folks getting jobs prior to the end of the disqualification period. A minority of folks state that they're trying to find work but can't find anything comparable to what they did before."

I went back to the city council and claimed that we seemed to be in a much worse unemployment situation than we had originally anticipated and I just couldn't see pulling the rug out from under these folks while they still can't find work. I proposed that the city council approve an extension of the Displaced Worker's Program from six months to one year. This time the city council voted 3-3. I had to cast the tie-breaking vote to pass the extension.

Sammy created a new table to show the budget impact with the Displaced Worker's Program benefits extended to 1-year.

Displaced Workers Program III (6-mo)		
Total Workforce		54,000
Unemployment Rate		6.0%
Disqualified		0.0%
Net Unemployed		6.0%
Unemployed Workers		3,240
Avg Annual Salary	$	55,000
Monthly Admin Cost	$	145,000
Monthly Cost	$	12,025,000

This time, I wanted to spend a little time getting a better sense of what was going on with the employment situation in our community. I met again with James Pennyworth at the Pirate's Cove Restaurant.

We exchanged the typical introductory chitchat and I then opened up the conversation. "James, it seems like the unemployment rate in our community has risen sharply in the past year. Are you experiencing this same problem at your paper mill?"

"We haven't laid any more people off than we would normally with our seasonal layoffs. However, it seems that when we have tried to hire people for very low-level positions, we're having problems finding interested workers. I hate to admit it, but I have had to hire some folks from Capital City as it's been hard to find workers here in Trial Town."

I was shocked. "James, that simply makes no sense. Trial Town's unemployment rate has risen from 4% when I talked with you six months ago; and now it's up to 6%."

Normally, James has some insightful words that help me see the error of some program that I've devised, but this time he was empty. "Arthur, I don't know what to tell you. You may want to talk with some of the folks who are not finding jobs and see what's going on."

As I got back into my car, I thought James was right. I had to talk with some of the people who couldn't find work. Maybe this would shed some light on the situation.

I talked with Sammy to get a few names of the people who had been receiving Displaced Worker's benefits for more than four months. Sammy was reluctant at first, as this information was confidential. However, he did manage to get two people to agree to meet with me to talk about their situation. Ralph Wiggins was laid off from James Pennyworth's paper mill six months ago. Sara Walton was let go from her job as a factory worker at the local plate factory. I first met with Ralph at Pirate's Cove.

After introductions, I started our conversation. "First of all, thank you for meeting with me, Ralph."

"Mayor, I'm always willing to help. Especially when there's free food involved."

I smiled at Ralph's remark. "Ralph, we seem to have an employment problem in Trial Town. I'm trying to get a better handle on what's causing the problem."

"Mayor, with all due respect, I'm not an employer. It seems like you may make more headway talking with the employers in our town. I think they know more about this crappy job market than I do."

"Ralph, I had a meeting with James Pennyworth at the paper mill. He doesn't seem to know much more than I do about what's causing the problem."

Ralph shrugged. "Well, if you ask me, Pennyworth is probably part of the problem. I worked at the paper mill for over two years. When things got a little slow, that SOB laid me off."

"Ralph, I think I got James' viewpoint. I'd now like to get your viewpoint on how your job search has been going."

"I've checked with the paper mill on a monthly basis to see if they have any job openings. There doesn't seem to be a job that's comparable to the job I had when I left."

"Okay. We're getting somewhere. What else have you been doing to find work?"

"I look at the Sunday paper every week. When I see a job that'll pay enough and is consistent with my experience and skill, I submit a resume and follow up with a phone call. I've only got two interviews in the last three months, and didn't get either job."

"If you don't mind me asking, what is your skill? And what was your annual compensation at your previous job at the paper mill?"

Ralph responded with pride, "I'm a mechanic. I'm good at fixing almost anything that breaks. That's why I don't understand why they let me go at the paper mill. I'm surprised that things work at all in that place without me."

I then prompted, "And your annual salary?"

Ralph was a little reluctant but then offered, "The paper mill took pretty good care of me. They paid me $100,000 per year in salary plus full health care benefits and a retirement program."

"Ralph," I prompted, "what if the Displaced Worker's Program runs out? It was initially supposed to last three months. We then extended it to six months; now we have extended this program to one year. What will happen if you don't have a job at the end of a year?"

Ralph responded, "Mayor, let me just say that the Displaced Worker's Program has been a life-saver for me. If that program didn't exist, I'd have most likely lost my house, lost my car and had to take some job serving fries to people in this restaurant."

I asked again, "Ralph, what will you do if you don't have a job at the end of a year in the Displaced Worker's Program?"

Ralph looked a little stressed. "Mayor, I'm honestly not sure what I'll do. I think that something decent should come along before that time, so I should be fine. If not, I guess I have my severance money from the paper mill. If I run out of those funds, I may be homeless."

"Ralph, I certainly hope it doesn't come to that. I really wish you the best of luck in your job search."

I set up a similar meeting with Sara Walton at the Pirate's Cove. Sara seemed like she was in great spirits when we met. I started our conversation. "Sara, you seem to be in a good mood. Did you find a job?"

"Oh no! I haven't found a job. No reason to be in the dumps about things."

"That's a good attitude. Sara, we seem to have an employment problem in Trial Town. Our unemployment rate has risen from 4% to 6%. I'm trying to get a better handle on what's causing this problem."

"How can I help? I'm just a laid-off plate factory worker."

"Sara, you've been unemployed for five months and I want to know how your job search has been going?"

Sara's sunny disposition changed to cloudy and she acted a little defensive. "I've been in touch with the Displaced Worker's Office on a weekly basis and they have a record of my attempt to find a job."

I hoped to break the ice a little. "Sara, I'm not saying that you aren't looking for a job but I am trying to get a better sense of why Trial Town employers aren't hiring people like you."

"Like I said, I've been getting at least one resume out a week. I have even had about six interviews. For some reason no one wants to hire me, so I keep up the routine."

Sara seemed a little reluctant to share information so I probed further. "Tell me about one of your interviews."

Sara resisted at first but then offered, "One of the interviews was with this restaurant, Pirate's Cove. I applied for a waitress job but they didn't offer me the job."

I was a little surprised. Sara seemed like a very personable woman and I thought she would have made a great waitress.

After we finished our meal, I thanked Sara for her time and being so forthcoming with how her job search was going. I wished her well and then decided I would hang around Pirate's Cove for a little while longer. I asked the hostess if the hiring manager was in the restaurant today. She acknowledged that she was. I asked if I could meet with her in private for a quick discussion. The hostess got the manager, Sherry Long, from the back.

I introduced myself, "Hi, Sherry, I am…"

Sherry interrupted, "I know who you are, Mayor. You've been coming in this restaurant for the past five years. What kind of restaurant manager would I be if I didn't recognize one of our best customers?"

I chuckled, "Of course. Do you have a few minutes for a conversation?"

"Sure. Our lunch rush is over, and I'm stuck in the back doing paperwork. I'd welcome a break."

We went into Sherry's paper-cluttered office and I opened the discussion. "Sherry, it seems that Trial Town is faced with an employment problem. I just had lunch with Sara Walton to discuss why she may be having problems finding work. I was wondering if you could answer a few questions about Sara's application for employment with your restaurant."

Sherry was caught off guard. "Mayor, we normally don't share any information regarding prospective employees or existing employees without their permission."

"Sherry, I appreciate your situation. However, I really need to figure out this employment problem and I have a sense that you can really help if you can share this information."

Sherry smiled. "Okay. I'm going to have you sign a confidentiality agreement that indicates that you can't share this information with anyone else without either my permission or Sara's permission."

I was glad to sign the agreement and then opened up the discussion. "Sara told me that she responded to an ad with your restaurant for a waitress position. She added that although she interviewed, she wasn't offered the job. I'm sure that you hired the right person, but it seems to me that Sara would have made a good waitress. Can you tell me why you didn't hire her?"

Sherry smiled again. "Mayor, the interview with Sara was a little odd. She did give us her resume and we felt she would be a good fit for the job. When I met Sara, I was convinced she would make a great waitress. However, during our conversation, she acknowledged that she responded to our newspaper ad and showed up to the interview as a condition of the Displaced Worker's Program."

"That's probably true. But I'm still wondering why you didn't hire her."

"That wasn't the only thing that Sara said. She indicated that after being let go from the plate factory, she and her husband agreed that Sara should stay home with their kids. Apparently her husband's income was enough to support them both as long as they controlled their spending habits."

I was confused. "So if that's what she wants to do, why is she looking for work and enrolled in the Displaced Worker's Program?"

Sherry smiled again. "Mayor, if someone paid you to pretend to look for work, wouldn't you keep the gig going for as long as you could?"

"I suppose so."

I was furious. Here I thought that Sara was actually trying, but just not having any luck finding a job. Now I find that Sara is just making some extra cash at Trial Town taxpayers' expense and doesn't intend to find a job.

I then asked, "Sherry, if Sara didn't indicate that she really didn't want the job, would you have hired her?"

"Yes. Sara seemed to be the most qualified. But as soon as she indicated she really didn't want the job, I didn't check references or pursue her employment any further."

I closed our conversation. "Sherry, you've been very helpful and I promise not to share Sara's information with anyone else."

I felt I had enough information to understand Sara's situation.

Sammy was able to set up a third meeting with just one more person who had just started participating on the Displaced Worker's Program. John Montgomery had worked at the local power plant for the past two years. He was laid off a few months ago. As with the other two, I set up a lunch with John at Pirate's Cove.

I opened my conversation with John just as I had opened my conversation with Ralph and Sara. "John, we seem to have an employment problem in Trial Town and I'm trying to get a better handle on what's causing the problem."

John replied, "I'd be glad to help in any way I can, Mayor."

"John, my first question is why did you lose your job at the power plant?"

John was very forthcoming. "Mayor, I was a mechanic on the steam turbine that's associated with one of the high-pressure coal steam boilers. The power plant is shifting over to natural gas turbines. With this switch, they need fewer coal boiler mechanics and so they let me go."

"So how's your job search coming?"

"I have several promising leads in the last two months. A few of these leads are for jobs that pay quite a bit less than what I was making at the power plant. But some job is better than no job."

"Can you tell me about the job leads?"

Again, John was accommodating. "Sure. One of the jobs is at the local hardware store. I'd help with stocking and do a weekly training class on plumbing. Another lead is a pipe fitter for a local mechanical contractor. If these two jobs fall through, I have heard that Pirate's Cove is hiring folks; so I may land a job here."

"John, you really don't seem to be that worried about job opportunities. You also don't seem to be too picky about the job you get."

"I'm forty-eight years old and have been in the work place for a long time. I knew that the job at the power plant wouldn't last long because I was aware that the new gas turbine technology was coming. It was just a matter of time before I was laid off. I've always saved enough money to pay my bills for at least six months if I were to lose my job. In fact, now I have saved up a years' worth of salary to pay bills, plus I was given another six months' severance pay from the power plant."

"It sounds like you don't even need the Displaced Worker's Program."

John was a little sheepish. "To be honest, Mayor, I feel this program is a waste of Trial Town's money. I understand that there may be some workers out there who have over-extended themselves financially, but I'm not sure that Trial Town should be responsible for paying for these folks."

"John, if you feel this is a waste of Trial Town's funds, why are you participating in the program?"

"I actually hadn't planned on participating. The Trial Town employee who called me convinced me that I would be a fool if I turned down this free money. I felt I had to take the money."

I thanked John for his input and wished him well in his job search.

I thought a lot about my discussions with John, Sara and Ralph.

Another six months went by and it was now officially a year since we started the Displaced Worker's Program. I asked Sammy if he could put together a table that showed the monthly cost of the program by month, the percent unemployment by month and the monthly and cumulative cost of the Displaced Worker's Program. He left the chart in my in-basket and I was simply shocked at what I saw.

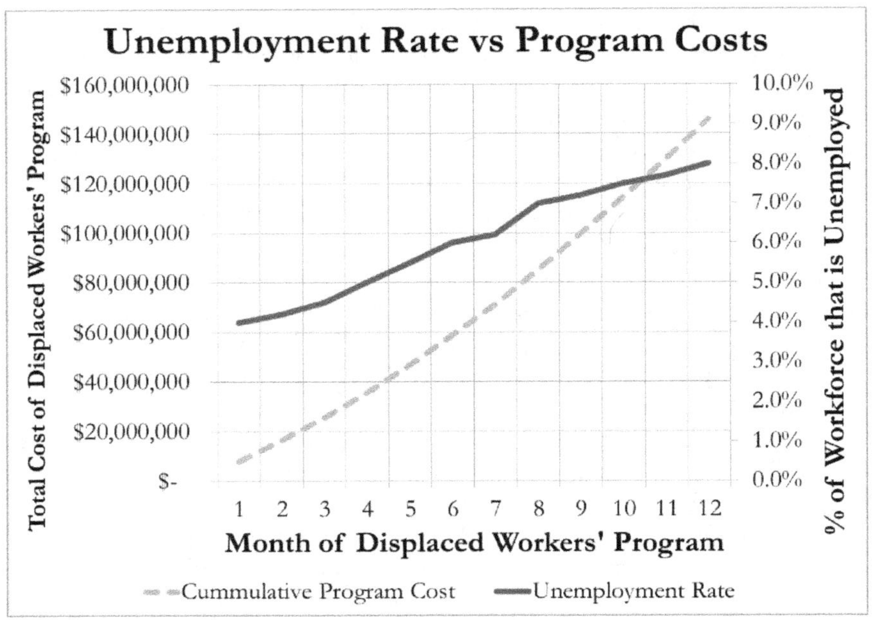

I noticed that our unemployment rate had been gradually rising over the year and the cost was really getting out of control. Our total cost had increased each month. The total for the year was a whopping $146 million. This had tapped all of Trial Town's cash reserves.

I thought about the conversations I had with Ralph, Sara and John six months before.

Ralph seemed to be a little fussy about the job that he would take in order to become employed again. I also thought that the Displaced Worker Program was probably helping Ralph justify accepting the 80% of the large salary that he had at the paper mill and not attempt to be employed at any lesser jobs.

I then thought about my conversation with Sara. Here was a person who was getting funds from Trial Town and never intended to find a job. That really made me mad.

Then I thought about John. Here was a person who had financially planned for a layoff and was already prepared for a duration of unemployment while he searched for his next job. John also seemed willing to take a job to provide for himself and his family that may pay less or not be in his chosen career. He would not have even signed up for the program if he had not been sold the free handout by one of Trial Town's employees.

I was certain that there were displaced workers who had a hard time finding a job after they had lost their initial job. Nevertheless, in the three interviews I had held, I couldn't see how the Displaced Worker's Program helped anyone. In fact, I think the program actually *rewarded* people who did not prepare for a new job search like John.

I also thought about my discussion with James Pennyworth. James indicated that he couldn't get Trial Town citizens to take lower paying jobs. I think this may have been because these folks were doing okay with 80% of their compensation with the Displaced Worker's Program. In fact, he was hiring Capital City citizens to do work that unemployed Trial Town citizens refused to do.

On top of all of these problems, the cost of the program would eventually become prohibitive. If the program had actually been serving a need in our community, we could have probably taxed employers to fund the program long-term; however, that would have taken even more money out of a stressed economy, meaning there would be even fewer jobs to offer to people who could work.

I had made some conclusions about the Displaced Worker's Program. The intention of the program was to be a safety net for workers who had lost their job at no fault of their own. Instead, the program was a disincentive for displaced workers to take lower paying jobs. It encouraged unemployment to rise and last longer than if these same workers accepted lower paying jobs. John had it right. He had taken the initiative to prepare for a possible layoff. He had reduced his expenses so that he saved enough to pay for his own Displaced Worker's Program. By Trial Town providing a safety net, we were discouraging people from being responsible. Considering Sara's situation, I felt we were paying people not to work who did not even intend to find employment.

I had my mind made up. I went to the city council and shared all of the data that Sammy had prepared for me regarding the financial performance of the Displaced Worker's Program. I also stated that I wanted to either eliminate it or change the program to fund unemployment benefits for a maximum of two months at 80% of a person's salary. Sammy provided more information and indicated that if we reduce the duration to two months, we would reduce the monthly amount paid from $16 million per month to $4 million per month. I did make one additional recommendation to keep the program funded long-term. I asked that the city council pass a tax called the Displaced Worker Tax, which would fund the $4 million per month cost so that Trial Town would not go into debt funding the program.

We had quite a heated discussion. The city council agreed to pass the Displaced Worker's Tax and we reduced the funded time from one year to two months.

Did I hear it the next day after our vote! I got calls from many angry citizens of Trial Town. I guess I should have expected that. Many folks had grown dependent on the Displaced Worker's Program. After considering the complaints, I decided to gradually reduce the duration of the Displaced Worker's Program from one year to two months over a two-year-period.

As time went on, our unemployment rate gradually decreased from 8% to 5%. It did not quite reach the 4% it had been before we started the Displaced Worker's Program. I always wondered if even the two-month-period was a disincentive for folks to find new jobs quickly. I felt if I went back to the city council to eliminate the two-month benefit, they would have a complete fit. So, I left well enough alone.

Real World Examples

Unemployment is an entitlement program in the United States that has been around since the Great Depression in 1930. The program is normally funded by employers purchasing unemployment insurance. This can be considered a tax but it's actually paid into a state pool. In some cases, funds are paid to a private insurance underwriter responsible for administering the unemployment insurance program. Unemployment insurance purchases are normally mandatory. To an employer, these costs are like a mandatory tax.

In 2009, our federal government passed the American Recovery and Reinvestment Act (ARRA) and funded a large increase in unemployment benefit programs from 26 weeks (6.5 months) to 99 weeks (almost two years). The financial crash in 2008 resulted in job losses and other economic problems that led to reported unemployment rates in excess of 14%. The unemployment rate was reported to have dropped to 7.2% in late 2013 as a result of the government's intervention. Non-corrected statistics show that the true unemployment rate was 12% prior to the economic problems in 2008; then skyrocketed to 20% and then gradually crept up to 24% after the increased duration of unemployment benefits offered as an ARRA benefit. This higher unemployment rate can be found on www.shadowstats.com. This rate includes those folks who have simply given up looking for work. This means that 7.2% of working class folks were getting unemployment benefits in 2013. However, an additional 13.8% of working class people either gave up looking for jobs or were not serious workers in the first place.

The one item in the Trial Town story that is different to our national picture is that unemployment benefits normally cap out at a rate that is below 80% of your actual income prior to being laid off. In Trial Town, when Ralph was laid off, he made 80% of his $100,000 per year salary, which would be $80,000 per year. However, in the real world, Ralph's unemployment benefit would have probably been capped at closer to $25,000 per year.

Unemployment insurance has helped create a culture of not saving or preparing for layoffs. All workers should put at least six-month's salary in a savings account in order to prevent a situation that requires government assistance.

10 SKY'S THE DEBT LIMIT

"America has a debt problem and a failure of leadership. Americans deserve better."
— Barrack Obama

We added several government services that were enjoyed by our citizens in Trial Town. We had a postal system, retirement programs, medical treatment services for the elderly, medical services for the poor, a financial support system for the poor, food payments for those who could not afford food, one of the most powerful military forces in the world, and many other programs that were the envy of the industrialized world. There was only one problem. We were taking in $1.2 billion per year in tax revenues but Trial Town's expenses had climbed to $1.6 billion per year. This meant that Trial Town was accumulating debt at a rate of $400 million per year.

I decided to set up a meeting with Ben Wellington, a very smart banker in Trial Town, to investigate some creative ways we could finance this deficit. We met at my usual favorite; Pirate's Cove. We got through the typical introductions and were ready to get down to business.

Ben started. "Arthur, you sounded a little frantic when you set up this meeting over the phone. Why do you want to talk with me?"

"Ben, Trial Town has been running into some financial difficulty. We have been losing $400 million in our budget each year. Your bank owns a lot of our debt. Honestly, if we keep this up, I'm concerned that we won't be able to pay you back."

Ben smiled. "That isn't the kind of talk a banker likes to hear."

"That isn't the kind of news I like to give. Do you have any ideas on what we can do better?"

"Have you thought about raising your revenues to match your expenses. Plus a little extra to help pay off your debt?"

"We already tax citizens and companies in Trial Town at a rate of 15%. I'm concerned that if we raise our tax rate higher, our economy will suffer. Plus, the city council members and I are quite concerned that if we raise taxes higher, we won't be re-elected in the next election cycle."

"Okay. Have you considered cutting your expenses to match your revenues?"

"People have become very dependent on the government programs we have developed. If we eliminate these programs, I think we will lose our bid for re-election when the time comes."

Ben interjected, "So, let me get this straight. It sounds like you want to run a budget shortfall indefinitely. How can that be sustainable?"

I responded rather sheepishly, "I understand our predicament. But I think that our economy may pick up at some point in the future and then we won't have this deficit. My hope is that this current annual shortfall is a temporary problem. Is there anything that you can do that can help us in our situation?"

"Let me think about it. I will see what I can do."

About one month after our meeting, Ben called me. "Arthur, I think I have an idea on how we can get Trial Town through the current financial difficulty. I'd like to meet you in your office to discuss this further."

I responded with enthusiasm. "That's great. I knew that you would figure this out. Please come down to my office this afternoon and we can discuss your plan."

We actually met in our conference room as Ben insisted that he would need an overhead projector. As I walked into the conference room, Ben already had his laptop computer and the following image projected on the screen.

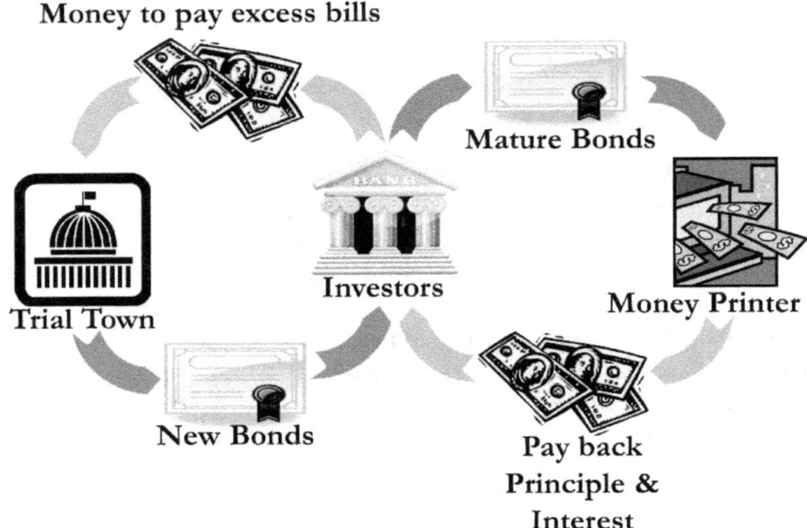

"Hi Ben, I am eager to see what you figured out on our debt problem."

Ben was beaming. "Mayor, I think this plan is simply brilliant."

"You sound optimistic. Let's hear your plan."

"Arthur, when Trial Town has a budget deficit; in other words, you spend more money than you take in; you will issue bonds to investors who are willing to fund Trial Town's debt."

I was somewhat disappointed in Ben's simple solution. "I don't really see how this is any different than the debt that we're now incurring from your bank. How in the world can we pay back this debt if we don't have the money once the bonds become due?"

Ben smiled. "That's the beauty of this plan, Arthur. Once the bonds mature and investors want their money, we simply print money to pay these investors."

I was amazed at the simplicity of Ben's plan. "We can just do that? Just print money to pay back this debt?"

"We have always printed money at the Money Printer for Trial Town. We have tried to limit the amount we print to allow only a modest growth in the amount of money that is in circulation but I don't see why we need to worry about printing a little more money to pay off these investors."

I was still a little confused. "So we can just print this money and Trial Town's debt just disappears?"

"It isn't quite that simple. Trial Town will still have debt but it can just re-issue this debt as new bonds. We cannot just erase Trial Town's debt. The city will still have the debt and it will still have to pay at least interest costs on its debt. However, Trial Town won't have to come up with any principle payments until the economy picks up and we can afford to pay down the principle amount of money."

I still needed clarification. "So, we will still have the same budget shortfall that we have now and keep these cycles repeating indefinitely?"

Ben looked a little concerned. "Mayor, you had indicated that you felt your financial situation was temporary. At some point, Trial Town will have to pay back its debts."

I was feeling a little more confident at this point. "Why do we need to ever pay it back? It seems like this cycle could go on indefinitely. Is there is a limit to how long this cycle can last?"

"Arthur, I will advise you like I would a home owner. My advice is that you should never have your amount of debt exceed four times your annual revenues. In the case of Trial Town, you can multiply $1.2 billion by four to get a total debt limit of $4.8 billion."

"Okay. I understand the limit. What will happen if investors don't want to buy our bonds?"

"Trial Town has a solid financial standing in the investor community. I think we will always be able to find investors. Especially when these investors understand we can always print more money to pay them back."

"What about the interest rate? What interest rate will we have to pay for this debt?"

"That's a good question, Arthur. If this debt lasts a while, a high interest rate can get you to your limit quickly. If other investment options are relatively limited, I believe that Trial Town will be able to get a very low interest rate on its bonds. In fact, I think we can set up a system in our money printing operation that establishes a low interest rate for all debt. That way Trial Town bonds will be very attractive."

I was confused again. "How can our Money Printer establish interest rates? I always thought that interest rates were a result of higher or lower inflation."

"Our Money Printer already provides loans to many banks within Trial Town, including my bank. Banks then loan this money out to other companies and people who want to borrow money. One of our bank's customers is Trial Town. The Money Printer loans money to a bank at say 1%, then banks loan this money to others at say 5%. That's how banks make money."

I was still confused. "I still don't understand. How can we tell the Money Printer the rate to charge others? I always thought that interest rates were dependent on inflation. In other words, if I have $10 today, it will be worth $20 next year if inflation is high and will be worth $10.10 next year if inflation is low."

"Arthur, that's certainly the way interest rates used to be set. However, if the Money Printer sets the interest rate, we will need to control this variable and avoid high interest costs for Trial Town."

After my meeting with Ben, I was still skeptical and somewhat confused by his money-printing plan, but I did not have any better answers. I brought Ben's idea to the city council. I believed that all city council members were as confused as I was on the repayment options. Nevertheless, they understood that if they reduced spending or increased revenues, they would lose their upcoming elections. The council voted to allow the money-printing system to operate as long as the council could vote on the limit of total money that could be borrowed. This limit would be known as the 'Debt Limit.' The city council set the Debt Limit at Ben's recommended amount of $4.8 billion.

We then put the plan into effect. Investors were very willing to buy our bonds and we were getting the low interest rate by convincing the Money Printer to keep interest rates low to all banks. I felt our plan was working extremely well. It almost felt we could spend whatever we wanted because we had a money machine that could support any amount of debt.

Unfortunately, our expenses never seemed to be lower than the tax revenues we were taking in and our debt had increased to $7 billion. Our city council seemed willing to increase our Debt Limit when we asked.

We were still spending about $400 million more per year than were taking in. Even though our money machine was working well, I was concerned there were some problems on the horizon.

Although I trusted Ben's advice, it seemed he was not an objective advisor. After all, Ben was making a lot of money in this money printing operation. I wanted to get an objective opinion about what we were doing with this money printing system.

Jarrod Fremont is the economics professor at our local college. I wanted to get his opinion on our money printing system. I met Jarrod in his office on the Trial Town College campus.

"Jarrod, thanks for meeting with me."

Jarrod remarked, "It's about time that you came to visit me, Mayor."

I was a little shocked. "What do you mean? I'll bet you don't even know why I'm here."

Jarrod stated confidently, "I know why you're here. It's because of this financial mess you're making for Trial Town. You want me to bail you out."

I was confused. "What do you mean financial mess? We've created an amazing system to fund Trial Town debt forever and ever."

"Really?"

"We have this financial system that seems like it can fund Trial Town's debt forever. We have affectionately called this system the money-printing system. However, I have an ominous feeling. Something feels wrong. It seems this system is just too good to be true."

"Mayor, you really don't know the problems you have created with your money-printing system, do you?"

"I guess not. What problems are you talking about?"

"Let me ask you a different question. What have you paid for a gallon of milk recently?"

I was taken by surprise. "I honestly have no idea. My wife does our grocery shopping so I really have not paid attention."

Jarrod smiled. "Let me help you out, Mayor. The price of milk is currently $4.00 per gallon."

I was so confused. "What in the world does the price of milk have to do with Trial Town's money printing system?"

Jarrod smugly asked another question. "Mayor, I'm guessing that you also don't know what the price of milk was just ten years ago when you started the money printing system?"

"You're right, I don't know. Nor do I see what any of this has to do with Trial Town's Money Printing."

Jarrod smiled. "The price of milk was $1.70 ten years ago."

I was still confused. "Can you please explain to me what the price of milk has to do with anything?"

"Mayor, I'm going to give you a quick lesson in economics. When Trial Town prints money with the Money Printer, you inject more money into the economy. Our community has a relatively fixed amount of goods to purchase. By necessity, the price of these goods has to increase."

I still was not tracking what Jarrod was saying. "Are you saying that by Trial Town printing money, we have caused the price of milk to increase?"

"Let's say that you have a single room. This room is your entire universe. In this room exists ten gallons of milk, owned by Joe. Also in this room is $10, owned by Jane. Joe wants to sell his milk and Jane wants to buy milk. In this simply universe, the cost of milk will be $1 per gallon. This is $10 divided by ten gallons of milk."

Jarrod continued. "Now let's say that another person in the room starts printing money and gives an additional $30 to Jane. By default, the price of milk just increased to $4 per gallon. This is known as inflation. When Trial Town prints money and injects it into Trial Town's economy, the cost of goods has to go up."

"What if Jane decides to continue to pay $1 per gallon and save the remaining $30?"

Jarrod smiled. "In the simple universe I described, Jane would have no reason to save the money because there is nothing else to buy. In the real world, Jane will try to pay as little as she can for milk. Likewise, Joe will try to charge as much as he can for his milk. Joe will use Jane's money to buy more dairy cows, feed, or energy to produce more milk. As the entire economic world is full of more money, Joe will also have to pay more for these items. He will then have to charge Jane more for the milk because he will get charged more for the supplies he needs to make milk."

I smiled. "So there is inflation… so what? Everyone pays more for things and everything works out."

"Mayor, things may work out if Trial Town was an isolated economy. However, Trial Town is in economic competition with other communities in the world."

I had to interject. "Jarrod, I really don't see what problems have been caused by this so-called inflation that you're going on about."

Jarrod calmly stated, "Mayor, are you aware that three of our Trial Town factories have moved their operations to Capital City?"

"I know the plate factory, stuffed bear plant, and the paper mill have moved some of their operations to Capital City. When I talked with these folks, they claim their profits are better than ever and their tax payments to Trial Town reflect this fact. So what if they have moved some of their operations to Capital City?"

"They moved these operations to Capital City because Capital City's work force is less expensive than ours. Capital City citizens don't have to pay high prices for general living expenses, so they need less compensation. You may be surprised to learn that the cost of a gallon of milk in Capital City is only $2.00 per gallon. Folks that used to work for these factories in Trial Town had to go onto the Displaced Worker's Program, food programs, housing programs and financial assistance programs, thus increasing Trial Town's expenses. Those who haven't been added to these social programs, move to Capital City because of its lower cost of living."

I rationalized the problem. "Trial Town may have a few more people needing government services and the cost of milk is higher than Capital City's, but I really don't see what options we have. If I cut government services, I won't make it through the next election cycle. If I try to increase taxes, it will probably hurt our economy more; plus everyone will be angry about paying more in taxes and not elect me the next election cycle."

"Mayor, do you understand you won't be able to continue this money printing operation indefinitely?"

"I think we can."

Jarrod breathed a big sigh and then started talking. "Mayor, I think you need more of an education in economics. There are four major risks if you continue your money printing operation. The first problem is that you'll continue to drive a portion of working class people into costly government support programs. Another portion of our working class folks will opt to work in places like Capital City where they can afford to support themselves financially.

"The second problem is that there is a limit to how much debt citizens of Trial Town will be able to realistically pay back in the future. Trial Town currently has $7 billion in debt and you are growing this debt by $400 million each year. Let's say that you could turn your annual budget shortfall into a surplus of $400 million per year. It will take 20 years to pay all of Trial Town's debt off at the current artificially low interest rate of 1%. If investors in Trial Town decide to start demanding a higher interest rate… let's say 5%, then it will take 45 years to pay this debt back. That's assuming you wake up and start cutting costs and raising revenue now."

I interrupted Jarrod. "What if we simply never pay back the debt or default to all of our investors?"

Jarrod smiled. "Mayor, if you default on Trial Town's debt, you will certainly lose your next election. Beyond that, you will damage Trial Town's ability to borrow funds in the future. At that point, you will be forced to eliminate your government services and you will still need to increase taxes to pay for whatever services you choose to provide. A default will result in a damaged credit rating and you will have to cut your costs anyway. Not to mention you'd have the legacy of leaving office with the price of milk four times what it was when you started this whole scheme."

I had never thought about the fact that we needed to end this debt situation. Jarrod made a compelling case. "I think I understand the down side now."

"You are creating a third problem with your money printing operation."

"It gets worse?"

"You're making Trial Town money worth less than other currencies in the world. By printing so much money, you have made most imported goods cost more. Other towns like Capital City are becoming much stronger than Trial Town as they are producing much more than our community."

I had to interrupt. "So what if other communities are manufacturing goods? As long as we keep the money printing operation going, our community members should have plenty of money to buy these goods."

Jarrod smiled. "It starts with manufacturing jobs. Trial Town will lose high paying labor-intensive jobs to automation, as companies cannot afford to pay high salaries. But they can afford to purchase low-cost machines from foreign manufacturing communities. Then local companies figure out ways to outsource service jobs as well. Trial Town consumers will be compelled to purchase low-cost goods and services from out-of-town communities."

"So you're saying that we will go from a manufacturing community… to a service community… to a pure consumer community?"

"Yes, Mayor, that is exactly what I am saying."

"Well I say… so what?"

Jarrod was noticeably frustrated. "Here's the 'so what.' If you only have consumers, no one is actually making any money except for the business owners who have outsourced their businesses. This means that Trial Town will get less in tax revenue, requiring more government services for laid off workers, making the debt problem even worse."

"Okay, I think I now see the damage that our money printing operation is causing to our local community and even our tax income picture."

Jarrod went even further. "One last problem…"

"You have even more bad news?"

"I believe this is the most important problem. This money-printing scheme is causing enormous debt that will take 20 to 50 years or more to pay back. With this kind of timeframe, you and I will not be paying back this debt. You are forcing our children and grandchildren to pay back debt for government services and benefits that we are receiving as adults now. This is simply unethical in my mind and something that any government leader should find shameful."

I was depressed. "I think I see the problems….

- We're causing local inflation, resulting in our citizens paying more for goods than others;
- We're losing several parts of our local economic strength to neighboring communities;
- We now have a community comprised of the very poor, who rely on government services, and the very rich who have outsourced all of our local jobs; and
- We are building up an enormous debt that will take several generations to pay back.

Do I have it right?"

"I think you finally understand the error of your ways."

"So, what do you propose we do? I can't raise taxes without ruining our economy and I can't cut spending without making many others angry."

"Mayor, you have to lead. You have to educate your city council and the public. Educate them the same way I have educated you here today. These concepts are not easy to understand for most people. You have to try to simplify these concepts. Regardless of whether or not you're successful in your explanations to the city council or the public, you have to act on this debt crisis. If you fail to act, the crisis will take care of itself, and it won't be pretty."

After my meeting with Jarrod, I felt sick to my stomach. All those years of building up debt and printing money. I had no idea that the free ride would ever end. The reality is that our economy has not gotten better over the past ten years. I always thought that we could continue to borrow money through Ben's system forever. I was now aware that I was causing pain to many Trial Town citizens. These poor folks were probably not even aware of what was causing our collective financial problems.

I thought, 'I could just press the reset button and get back to where we started ten years ago and simply get our spending under control.' I was convinced that pressing the reset button was just too easy. I felt we had to figure out a way to get our finances back in order the old-fashioned way. We had to pay down our debt and get our budget situation fixed.

I proposed to our city council that we cut spending by $400 million per year to close the budget gap. I also proposed that we increase our income tax from 15% to 22% to increase revenues by $400 million per year. If this action did not tank the economy, it would provide a budget surplus of $400 million per year. At the end of 20 years, when our debt was paid off, I fully anticipated reducing our income taxes back to 15% and maintaining the budget discipline that I now knew was a necessity.

I also proposed that we pass a law that does not allow the city to spend more its income in any year unless there is a demonstrated national emergency. Such excess expenses would need to be approved by all members of the city council.

When I presented my plan to the city council, I did my best to educate them on the situation. I even brought Jarrod Fremont to the meeting to give our council the same lecture he gave me. My city council was furious. First, they did not understand why I wouldn't simply press the reset button to erase our large debt. They were further angered by the fact that I had misled them for ten years on our money-printing plan. It seemed like all of Trial Town was angry with me. Some were angry for me misleading them for ten years; some were angry for the programs that would have to be cut; others were upset about the proposed tax increase. Even some investors were upset that our bonds would be declining over the next 20 years as they had gotten used to putting their money into the money-printing program. Oddly, even though I knew I was proposing the right thing, I don't think I had one friend when I presented my plan to the city council.

Thankfully, three members of the city council agreed with me that we needed to get our financial act together regardless of the pain that we would inevitably feel for making this decision. The city council voted 3-3 to pass my proposal. I then cast the tie-breaking vote to pass my proposal in its entirety.

When re-election time rolled around, I barely kept my position as mayor. Unfortunately, the other three council members who supported me in the vote to end the money-printing program did not get re-elected. I spoke with each of them after their election losses and each one indicated that they were very proud of their vote to support fixing our financial situation. Trial Town citizens may never appreciate how we helped them.

It took 20 years. During that time, the city council tried to over spend or claim they needed emergency funds for frivolous spending. The law that was passed when I was in office prevented the overspending from ever happening. Over the years, Trial Town's inflation got back down to normal levels and many of our factory jobs returned to Trial Town.

Many business owners who had to pay higher taxes did fine and our economy did not tank. When I talked with the company owners, they claimed they had actually been quite concerned about the high debt that Trial Town was accumulating, as they believed that taxes would need to be levied to pay the high debt. They were okay with the higher income taxes as long as Trial Town vowed to eventually decrease tax rates, cut excessive spending and get its financial act together.

My personal advice to any other government leader who reads my book is:

- Don't get into debt if you can avoid it.
- Only borrow money for one-time emergencies, and not annual budget problems.
- If you have to borrow money, make sure you have a plan to pay it back as soon as you can.
- Printing more money digs the hole deeper. Don't do it.

My personal advice to citizens who have elected officials to represent them in government:

- Educate yourselves on basic economic principles.
- Understand the negative impacts of debt and money printing.
- Don't vote for politicians who promise you something for nothing.
- Never believe that money printing and run-away debt are ever acceptable government policies.

Real World Examples

The Trial Town story is very similar to the story of the US debt situation. At the writing of this book, the US debt is at $18.5 trillion and continues to grow by close to $2 billion per day (2015). Our government spends $3.9 trillion per year and takes in $2.3 trillion per year in taxes. The US is in the same predicament as Trial Town. If we cut our current expenses by $1.3 trillion per year and increase taxes by $500 billion per year, we could pay down our debt in the next 20 years. This debt repayment does not count the other liability problems the United States has with Social Security and Medicare. If you add these liabilities into the debt picture, it has been estimated that this increases our $18.5 trillion to $150 trillion. This amount of debt is hard for many folks to understand. $150 trillion in debt is not an amount of money the US economy can pay back in any time duration. In addition to our national debt, all US citizens also have local government debts they need to pay for new schools, city halls and other government obligations. In addition to this debt, most consumers borrow money to pay for cars, homes, land, student loans, etc.

The US debt situation is a little more complicated than the scenario described in Trial Town. Like Trial Town, the US also has a money printing operation called the Federal Reserve. The Federal Reserve prints money to pay back government bondholders, just like the Money Printer in the Trial Town story. Also, like the Trial Town story, the Federal Reserve attempts to keep interest rates at a very low level to try to reduce the US debt concerns as much as possible. Due to the amount of money printed over the past ten years by the Federal Reserve, inflation is now influencing the cost of living for all Americans.

If you analyze estimated inflation, otherwise known as the Consumer Price Index (CPI), we had relatively low inflation in the United States prior to the development of the Federal Reserve in 1913.

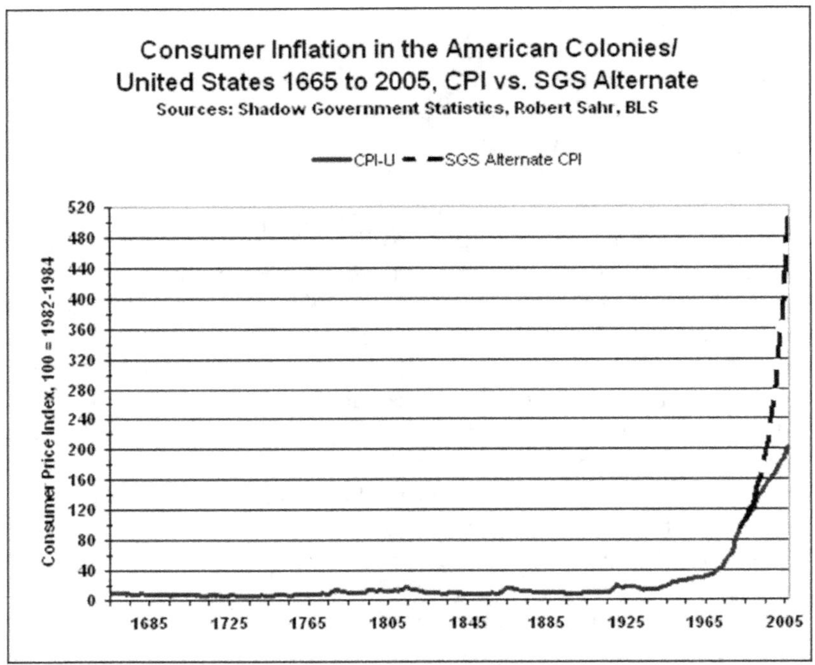

Since we have invented a way to make as much money as we would like, inflation has been out of control.

If you try to earn money in your savings account, they will probably pay you 0.1% interest per year. Essentially, you cannot get a pay raise and you cannot make money on your savings. Yet the cost of all goods and services are rising at a rate of 10%. This means that you are getting relatively poorer by an average of 9% per year. It is no wonder that many working class people cannot afford to pay their bills and both Mom and Dad need to work. Now adult children are living at home. Like Trial Town, the United States has become a nation of wealthy business owners, working middle class who are getting poorer by the day, and a dependent class who rely on government programs to survive. The only way our government can get out of this mess is by cutting its expenses drastically and cutting many of the income tax loopholes that currently exist for the wealthy. The US will need to collect taxes from all citizens regardless of income status.

The alternative for the US is the same fate that would have eventually faced Trial Town. If the US defaults on its debt, the value of our dollar will diminish and we won't be able to afford our government services anyway. Either way, the US will get to the same place. It is now just a matter of being proactive or allowing the inevitable crash to happen.

11 BREAD IS TOO EXPENSIVE!

" Shortages where the government sets prices have been common in countries around the world, for centuries on end, whether these shortages have taken the form of waiting lists, black markets, or other ways of coping with the fact that what people demand at an artificially low price exceeds what other people will supply at such prices."
—Thomas Sowell

Things were going relatively well in Trial Town. The one thing that bothered me was that some products seemed to be reasonably priced and other items seemed to be excessively expensive for most people. One of the items of concern for me was bread. Bread prices had increased from $0.75 per loaf up to $1.00 per loaf in the last five years. I felt our bread manufacturers were overcharging the consumers in Trial Town. It seemed like there was no way bread should cost so much. As the mayor, I thought there must be something I could do. Then it came to me. I can regulate the price of bread to be $0.80 per loaf and that will force bread makers of Trial Town to sell bread at a more reasonable price. Three bread-making companies resided in Trial Town: Baker's Bread, Trial Town Bread, and Best Bread.

I went to the city council to run my idea past council members and get their official approval.

Paul Fredrick reacted with anger. "Mayor, this is outrageous. This is a form of communism that I feel can be damaging to Trial Town."

As soon as Paul had stopped talking, Sally Hatfield spoke up. "I for one, feel you are on the right track. If this was a new car or something that people don't need, then I might agree with Paul but bread is a necessary food for all people. The high cost of bread affects poorer people and they can't afford to feed their families."

I had drafted a law that supported my bread control idea. I called it the "Bread Control Act." I felt it was time to put the Bread Control Act (BCA), regulating the price of bread below $0.80 per loaf, up for vote; it was passed 4-2.

I was gloating over my success of the BCA in my office on a relatively quiet afternoon. I had little work to do and no meetings. I was just getting ready to go home early and stop for the day, when I heard the distinct ring of my office phone. I was tempted to ignore the call and let it go to voicemail… but I picked it up. "Hello, this is Mayor Wallaby."

There was no immediate response and then I heard, "Hi, Mayor, it's Cal Hartman."

Cal Hartman is the owner of Baker's Bread. I had never met him in person, but I had heard from many folks in Trial Town that he was a good and respected businessman. After passing the BCA, I rather knew that some of the bread company owners would be upset. With some apprehension in my voice, I said, "Hi Cal. What can I do for you?"

"Mayor," Cal said angrily, "what were you thinking about regulating the price of bread from $1.00 per loaf down to $0.80 per loaf? How are we supposed to make any money at that low price?"

Hearing Cal's angry tone, I got a little upset myself. "Look, Cal. You greedy bread companies have had it too good for too long. It's about time someone stepped in and forced you all to sell bread at a reasonable price to Trial Town's citizens."

Cal got even angrier. "Mayor, it costs me $0.80 per loaf to make a loaf of bread. I then sell the loaf of bread to the grocery store for $0.95 per loaf to recover some overhead and make a small profit. The grocery store then sells the bread to the consumer at $1.00 per loaf to make some profit themselves. How do you propose we get the cost of our bread lower when we feel we are making bread at the lowest possible cost now?"

I responded, "Cal, you bread makers are going to have to figure that out.

Only five years ago, bread was at $0.75 per loaf so I am sure you can figure out how to get bread back down to a reasonable price."

Cal hung up his phone receiver without saying goodbye. I guess I should have expected some anger from these greedy bread makers because they would no longer be able to rake in their big profits.

Very shortly after the BAC went into effect, one of the bread makers, Trial Town Bread, decided to close their doors. I set up a meeting with the owner of Trial Town Bread, Phil Smith, to better understand his situation. We met at our typical spot, Pirate's Cove Restaurant.

Phil is a forty-something man who had always been a soft spoken, respected member of the Trial Town community. Phil had a wife of twenty years and three daughters. He was the stereotypical family man and everyone loved this guy.

After the typical introductions and small talk about the weather, I started our conversation. "Phil, I heard you are closing down Trial Town Bread as a result of the new BAC. Can you tell me if this is true?"

Phil sighed. "Mayor, it's true. We're barely making money at the current price of bread at $1.00 per loaf. The cost of making our bread is $0.90 per loaf. If the retail price of bread is $0.80 per loaf, there's simply no way we'll be able to make money."

I was a little confused. Phil did not seem as angry as Cal but rather content with his decision to close his bread factory. I had to ask, "Phil, isn't there some way that you can reduce your costs so that you can make a little less money than you did before?"

Phil smiled. "Look, Mayor, I was having a hard time as it was competing with Baker's Bread and Best Bread. I know what it took to get our bread price low enough to compete. If I have to drop another $0.20 per loaf, I'll be losing money hand over fist."

I was still a little confused by Phil's decision. "So why didn't you try to sell your bread-making company to Best Bread or Baker's Bread?"

Phil laughed. "Mayor, as soon as the BCA passed, bread companies were not exactly in high demand for most corporate buyers. A company is valued based on its ability to generate profit. After the BCA, our company would generate a loss of about $1 million per year. Not exactly a sellable company."

"Okay, Phil. What about your employees? Are you just going to lay them off?"

Phil was not so relaxed once I asked this question. I noticed a few tears welling up in his eyes. "Mayor, I'm truly heartbroken about having to lay off my employees. I have tried to give them a few months' pay to help out, but that's about all I could do."

It was apparent that Phil had made up his mind and that was just the way it was.

The next time I went to the grocery store, I noticed that there was no more Trial Town Bread on the shelf. In fact, it seemed like there was not much bread on the shelf at all.

I had discussions with Cal Hartman and Phil Smith but I did not have a chance to talk with Steve Merrick, the owner of Best Bread. I set up a meeting with Steve to discuss his perspective on the BCA, once again at the Pirate's Cove restaurant.

I did not know Steve well, but had heard that he was quite a shrewd businessman. In my discussions with Phil, he indicated that Steve was quite creative in finding a way to make a buck. Steve was in his early forties and had a confident, athletic appearance. He was recently divorced and had no children. Rumor was that Steve was married to his work.

When we met at the Pirate's Cove, Steve appeared to be in a similar mood as Phil Smith. However, I was almost certain that Steve had not decided to sell or close his company. I started the conversation. "Steve, I've already spoken with Cal Hartman at Baker's Bread and Phil Smith at Trial Town Bread. I wanted to get your feedback on the Bread Control Act that was recently passed."

Steve smiled. "Well, Mayor, as you can imagine, I'm not a fan. But I feel I have some ways to still make money with the lower bread price so Best Bread should do fine."

I then asked, "So, Steve, what does it cost Best Bread to make a loaf of bread?"

Steve smiled again. "Nice try, Mayor. I can't share that information with you. If I tell you how much it costs for us to make a loaf of bread, you could share this information with my competition and I'd be in trouble."

I then got it. "Okay, Steve. Sorry about that."

I was happier when I left my discussion with Steve convinced that these greedy bread companies COULD lower their prices.

Three months after the passage of the BCA, the news that I should have predicted started hitting the newspapers. Best Bread and Baker's Bread announced a layoff of 100 employees between them. I noticed in the grocery store that there were fewer loaves of bread on the shelves, but there were more hot dog buns and other baked goods, which seemed to be more expensive than I remembered.

I asked one of the grocery store clerks, "Say, why are there so few loaves of bread on the shelves?"

The clerk replied, "Well, we just don't get much bread delivered to our store any longer. In fact, these shelves are normally empty by noon each day. I think some folks are buying all the bread up in the morning and then they try to resell it."

"Son, if people are reselling bread for more than $0.80 per loaf, they are breaking the Bread Control Act and should be reported to the police."

The clerk shrugged and smiled. "Okay, mister. Good luck catching them!"

I was more than a little miffed. These bread company owners were probably just mocking me. They thought that they could just stop making bread and make citizens angry enough to fire their mayor. I decided I would teach them a lesson. We would enforce a higher production level of bread by law so that the bread companies would have to make enough bread.

I then proposed my idea to the city council. I told them that I wanted Best Bread and Baker's Bread to be forced to make a minimum number of loaves of bread equal to our previous production levels, as there was clearly not enough bread for citizens of Trial Town. I got a little more argument this time around.

Paul Fredrick reacted immediately. "Mayor, I think you're off your rocker. You are telling companies to produce more products at a lower price. These companies will most likely go out of business altogether. What if the bread companies simply decide not to make bread at all?"

I responded, "Paul, if the bread companies don't make loaves of bread, we will fine them an amount of money that will be comparable to the profit that they would have made on bread."

Paul followed with another question. "Mayor, what if the grocery store doesn't buy all the bread that the bread companies are producing?"

I was caught a little off guard by this question. "Well, I guess Trial Town will purchase any bread that can't be sold by the grocery stores."

Paul wasn't giving up on his questions. "Mayor, how is Trial Town going to pay for all this excess bread?"

"Paul, there won't be excess bread. Trust me, if you saw how bare those shelves in the store are recently, there won't be any left. Plus, since bread costs less, consumers ought to be buying more bread than the minimum production levels we've set."

Sally Hatfield then chimed in. "Well, Mayor, I for one think that you're the hero of the downtrodden. These greedy companies are holding us all hostages with their silly games. I'm glad someone is trying to hold these greedy companies accountable."

We held a vote to amend the Bread Control Act to include the production levels and called the new law the Bread Control Act II (BCA II). The city council voted 3-3 and then I cast the deciding vote to pass BCA II.

After the law passed, Cal from Baker's Bread did something that I would have never expected. Cal sold his baked goods division, which included everything, but loafed bread to another company called Baker's Goods. He sold his loafed bread division to Best Bread. Best Bread now had a monopoly on all of the loafed bread production in Trial Town. I thought this was probably okay. After all, Trial Town had now regulated the quantity and the price for loafed bread, so we had all the bases covered.

Again, there were more layoffs in the bread industry. I guess I should have expected this as well. Although I was not sure how Best Bread would make enough bread to meet their bread quotas with fewer workers. Oh well, that was their problem.

I then had an occasion to visit the grocery store to see how BCA II was affecting loafed bread inventory levels. When I entered the bakery department of the store, I was happy to see full shelves of loafed bread all priced at $0.80 per loaf. I was convinced that I truly was the hero that Sally thought I was. We had plenty of bread and it was all being sold at $0.80 per loaf.

I noticed the same store clerk was present. "Say, son, what do you think about having enough bread to sell?"

"Mister, that's certainly better than it was. But we have to throw away almost half of that bread every day."

"What? Why are you throwing away so much bread?"

"Have you tasted this bread, mister?"

"Not recently. I guess I better buy a loaf." I picked up a loaf and took it home.

When I opened the packaging, I noticed that the bread was somewhat stale smelling. I then buttered a piece and took a bite. It was probably the nastiest bread I had ever tasted in all my life. It tasted stale and there was a fine residue in the bread, like sawdust or something. The residue seemed to sit in my mouth and had no taste. I needed to meet with Steve Merrick to see what kinds of tricks he was playing.

I called him. "Steve, its Mayor Wallaby."

Steve answered, "Hi, Mayor, what can I do for you?"

"Have you tasted your bread lately?"

Steve laughed. "Nasty, isn't it?"

I was a little angered by Steve's cavalier response. "So, how do you expect anyone to buy your bread?"

"Honestly, Mayor, I wouldn't advise anyone to purchase our loafed bread. Like I said, it isn't that good."

I was so angry I was ready to throw my phone across the room. "Steve, what are you trying to pull here?"

Steve got a little more serious. "Look, Mayor, you first mandated a fixed price for a loaf of bread. This resulted in us bread companies laying off employees and simply producing less loafed bread. This, in combination with Trial Town Bread going out of business, resulted in a shortage of bread. Even with the lower production, Baker's Bread struggled to make a profit."

I was confused. "I don't get it, Steve. If bread prices drop, it seems like you would need to make more bread in order to make the same profits you made before."

Steve laughed. "Mayor, when you're making money on a product, you want to make as much as you can. However, we were losing money on loafed bread and so the less we produced the less loss we would have to offset with our other profitable products."

"But, Steve, why didn't you reduce your cost of bread making so that you could still make a profit on loafed bread?"

"Mayor, we did reduce costs. We lowered the wages of bakers and other workers that worked on loafed bread. These workers would either quit or try to get a job making other products that weren't cost-controlled. We did lower costs somewhat but there was no way we could match our production before the BCA was passed."

I was getting a little annoyed with Steve. "So, why are you making that crap that you are trying to pass off as bread in our grocery stores?"

"Mayor, when you ask a company to make a certain quantity of a product and you mandate a price that is lower than it takes for that company to make a profit, the only factor that can be changed is the quality of the product."

Steve continued. "When Cal and I heard about the mandated production levels, we put our heads together to figure out how we could both do okay in this new environment. Cal decided he couldn't make an inferior product and so he sold his bread loaf operations to me. I decided to make an inferior product in order to meet production levels and the mandated price levels."

"How did you reduce the bread quality and still call that crap bread?"

Steve was a little embarrassed, but continued. "Instead of using the wheat kernel to make flour, we realized that we could double flour production by milling the shaft of the wheat in addition to the kernel. We also use filler in the dough to make more bread."

I was a little upset, thinking about the inferior bread product that Steve was trying to push on our citizens. "How did you think any consumer would buy this product?"

"Mayor, I didn't need to worry about consumers purchasing our product. You forced the grocery stores to buy our product regardless of quality. You then promised the grocery stores that Trial Town would purchase any unsold bread loaves."

I was now livid. "Steve, I'll tell you what I am going to do…"

Steve cut me off. "Mayor, I already know what you are going to say and I would not advise it."

"Okay, smarty! What was I going to say?"

"You are going to tell me that you're now going to regulate the quality of the bread. Then you are going to think that you are controlling the quantity, price and quality and there's no other way for us bread companies to take advantage of Trial Town or bread consumers."

"So what if I do that? How are you going to work your way out of that regulation?"

"Mayor, I hope you don't do that, but I can't tell you what I would do."

I had had it with Steve. "Steve, if you don't tell me, I'll make my proposition to the city council. If you tell me, I may be persuaded to stop my plea."

Steve still seemed reluctant but said, "Mayor, if you mandate price, quality and quantity, I will be forced to sell off our loafed bread concern to a separate company and then file for bankruptcy. I'll probably maintain ownership of my other baked goods and simply lay off the rest of my workforce. Then Trial Town will have no loafed bread at all."

My face was noticeably a deep shade of red as I was now beyond angry. "Steve, I'll need to think about this a little more. Thank you for your time." I then slammed the phone onto the receiver.

After I had calmed down somewhat, I thought I would set up a time to meet with James Pennyworth, the owner of a local paper mill. I had known and trusted James for a long time. He had always given me good advice when I struggled to understand these greedy business owners. I met James at the Pirate's Cove.

I started the conversation. "James, have you heard much about the Bread Control Act we passed in Trial Town?"

James smiled. "Yes, Arthur, I've heard about the BCA and the BCA II."

"Good… that may make this conversation go better. You may also know that Best Bread now has a monopoly on loafed bread and they are making god-awful bread. Furthermore, because of the BCA II, Trial Town is now buying this bread because no person in their right mind would eat that crap."

James laughed. "Arthur, what did you expect?"

I was taken aback. "James, this isn't funny. How can we get out of this situation and get Best Bread to do the right thing and make quality bread at a low price?"

James smiled. "Arthur, you can't get high quality bread at a low price unless you repeal the BCA and the BCA II."

I was surprised. "What? I thought you would tell me some creative law that we could enact to make Best Bread fall in line. I simply hate that smug

Steve Merrick and would like him to get with the program."

James was now more serious. "Arthur, you don't understand how the free-market works."

"I think I know just fine. You are all trying to make as much money as you can off poor people who can't afford your products."

"Arthur, you're right that us company owners are trying to make a profit. We need these profits to reinvest into our companies to grow them. We have also risked a lot of our own wealth in the hopes of getting some of this money back in the form of profit. In the majority of cases, startup companies don't make a profit and they quickly go out of business."

"Okay, I guess profit is not bad. But what could we do to get bread prices down?"

James responded. "Arthur that's what you don't understand. The highest possible quality product at the lowest possible price is guaranteed in the free-market. When we had three bread companies, they had to compete against each other to sell their products. Consumers were buying the bread that was being supplied in the grocery stores. This was an equal balance of supply and demand."

The light started to come on for me. "So why would the lower price mess up this balance?"

"Arthur, when you forced a lower price with the BCA, demand went up. Unfortunately, supply diminished because bread makers couldn't make sufficient profits to motivate them to meet the demand. Since they couldn't make money on loafed bread, they decided to raise prices on other baked goods. They invested their resources into more profitable bread production to make up for the losses they were suffering on loafed bread."

I now understood. "So Trial Town increased consumer demand by forcing prices lower. Bread companies lowered supply as the lower price was not desirable. This increased demand and reduced supply, created massive shortages in grocery stores. That's why the shelves were empty."

"That's exactly right, Arthur."

"So, what about the poor quality bread that we have now?"

"Arthur, do you really have to ask? Okay… so you told bread companies they had to increase production levels and you told them that they still had to sell bread at the low price. What did you think would happen? The only option that bread companies had was to reduce the quality of their bread to keep their companies in business. You then guaranteed that Trial Town would purchase any unsold bread."

"James, what if I mandate a higher quality of bread?"

James laughed. "Arthur, you just want to keep digging this hole deeper, don't you?"

"I don't understand."

"Mayor, if you mandate quality, price and quantity, you will put any business owner in an impossible situation. The bread companies would have no alternative but to close their businesses."

"So what do you suggest?"

James was now getting impatient. "Arthur, I told you that you should repeal your ridiculous BCA laws."

"But, James, the price of bread will probably go back up to $1.00 per loaf."

James smiled. "My guess is that the price may even go higher as you have completely disrupted the bread business. Trial Town Bread went out of business. That's one less competitor in the market place. Baker's Bread sold their loaf-making division to Best Bread and so there's no competition in the bread business. This will allow Baker's Bread to charge whatever price they want until they hit competition from Capital City or elsewhere."

After my conversation with James Pennyworth, I was embarrassed about how much of a mess I had made out of Trial Town's bread business. All I had wanted to do was reduce the price of a loaf of bread and now citizens of Trial Town had crappy bread that no one wanted to buy. Our Trial Town government was losing money due to the massive layoffs, reduced taxes on profits and purchasing a lot of crappy bread that ended up in the dumpster.

James was right. With cost control came shortages, and then with mandated supply came poor quality. I guess the old free-market system with no government intervention was probably as good as it gets.

I educated the city council on my discussion with James and proposed that we repeal BCA and BCA II and not replace them with any regulations on the bread business. Sally Hatfield still thought the cheaper, nasty bread for the poor was better than the poor going hungry. I doubted that poor people would really "go hungry." The city council voted 4-2 to repeal both laws.

As James predicted, the price of bread immediately rose to $1.25 per loaf as Best Bread had a monopoly on loafed bread sales in Trial Town. However, Capital City bread companies quickly jumped into the market with the higher bread prices. This added competition forced prices to drop to $1.15 per loaf. A year after we repealed the laws, Trial Town Bread re-opened to compete in the newly formed bread market and prices dropped to $1.05 per loaf. We never got back down to $1.00 per loaf. However, I did learn a valuable lesson. Don't mess with the free-market. The free market will guarantee the lowest prices with the highest quality. I now feel I can buy bread in Trial Town and enjoy eating it.

Real World Examples

There are several examples where the United States government and other governments have tried to control costs of various items. Many electric utilities in the United States are regulated, allowing a single electricity company to provide electricity with prices established by a Public Utility Commission. Some states have deregulated their electricity markets and consumers are getting much more competitive prices for electricity. This is the opposite result as what we witnessed in the Trial Town Bread Price Control.

Many cities and other housing units in the United States have attempted to control the maximum price that can be charged for rent in select apartment complexes in an attempt to ensure that there is always affordable housing. These rent-controlled apartments are in a poor state of maintenance and some have been closed down or demolished. Other apartment complexes in these same cities are not controlled and cost more but have a waiting list for tenants, as they are much better apartments.

The U.S. government is heavily involved in controlling prices for agricultural commodities. Milk is one product that is heavily subsidized in order to keep the price of milk lower for consumers. The U.S. government is also heavily trying to control the price of wheat, corn, soybeans, rice, sugar, cotton and other agricultural commodities. In many cases, the government pays farmers not to grow crops for fear that prices for certain commodities will go too low.

The only way that government can help ensure the best possible prices on any item or service is to encourage a free-market. When a government imposes cost controls, one of two things will happen: 1) prices will be higher than what the free-market can provide through competitive selection by consumers; or 2) quality will be reduced to accommodate a lower-than-market price. Either result is not desired by most consumers.

12 GUNS = VIOLENCE

"One man with a gun can control 100 without one."
—Vladimir Lenin

Things were going well in Trial Town. Our finances were in control, the city council was getting along, and I was getting bored with my job. With a lull in the action, I decided to take a week off and catch up on work around the house.

It was a Monday and I was relaxing at my home, just enjoying the view from my deck, when the phone rang. I ignored it the first few times, but picked it up the third time. It was apparent that someone really wanted to reach me. It was Craig Boston, our chief of police.

He sounded frantic. "Mayor, have you been watching the news this morning?"

I calmly replied, "Craig, I'm taking a week off. I have tried to stay away from the news as much as possible this week."

Craig now sounded somewhat annoyed. "Mayor, we're having a major crisis in our city right now. A gunman opened fire in Anderson's Grocery Store and killed three people then killed himself."

I could feel the blood drain from my face. I literally felt sick to my stomach. At first, I thought that I did not hear Craig right. "Did you just say that someone killed three people in Anderson's Grocery Store?"

"Yes, you heard me right. Mayor, it's worse than that. Ten more people are in critical condition at our local hospital. In addition to the three victims, the gunman killed himself. We're now getting a warrant to search the gunman's home to see if we can find out why this guy committed this horrible act."

"I guess my vacation is over. Where'll you be? I would like to know information when you know it. I'm sure the press will want answers."

"I will be at the scene of the crime at the grocery store for at least the next hour. I've given some basic information to the press. I haven't given out the identification of the shooter or the victims. Unfortunately, it didn't take the press long to figure out who they were anyway. The press agreed to withhold names of the victims until we have notified family members."

"Chief, I'll get ready and meet you at the grocery store in the next thirty minutes."

As I was getting dressed, I was trying to wrap my mind around the situation. I was still in a state of disbelief. I just never thought an incident like this could ever happen in Trial Town.

When I arrived at the scene of the crime, my disbelief turned into horror and sadness. I noticed a bullet hole in the front glass as I entered the grocery store. I then got beyond the police tape and found Craig. He was hunched over a body next to a drying puddle of blood. I felt extremely nauseous. I think that I needed to see the damage that was caused so that I could better understand how real this tragedy was in our hometown. I had viewed these sights on my television about other communities, but I had never really understood the level of tragedy, until I experienced the situation first hand.

As I was joining Craig, I heard a flurry of activity and some shouting. Before I knew it, Martha Main, the reporter from TV-4, had her microphone in my face. A cameraman right behind Martha made sure the camera lights were shining in my eyes. Here came the questions.

"Mayor, what are your thoughts on this horrible tragedy?"

"Mayor, what is Trial Town going to do to prevent tragedies like this one?"

"Mayor, did you know any of the victims?"

"Mayor, did you know the shooter?"

I was not aware, but there were tears coming down my face. I was in no condition for a TV interview. I wiped the tears from my face and calmly responded to Martha, "Martha, I have only learned about this tragedy in the last hour. We still have many unanswered questions about exactly what happened. Once I have accurate information, I'll be in a better position to answer your questions."

Martha seemed to understand, and moved her attention to other people who had been present during the event. Chief Boston had already collected most of the eyewitnesses in a private space in the storage room of the grocery store. This meant that Martha would have to wait to get a meaningful story.

Craig left the crime scene to the investigators and the crime lab. He and I joined his detectives in the interview room. Given the situation, the eyewitnesses were relatively calm.

Sally Kraft was a cashier. She had huddled behind her counter in an attempt to stay out of the line of fire. Mark, a fellow cashier, had been shot and killed. As Sally was huddled behind her cashier stand, she could only hear the tragedy once the shooter started shooting.

I listened to Sally's story and that of the many other eyewitnesses who were in the grocery store. All of the stories were helpful in understanding what happened, but nothing seemed to answer my main question: Why did this happen?

This question stuck in my head when I first heard the news… and continued to echo in my mind for a week after the tragedy.

Chief Boston did uncover the basic facts about the shooter. He seemed to be angry at many things and was somewhat psychologically unbalanced. There was still no reason that made sense to me. We uncovered a letter the shooter had left in his home, but it really did not add much to explain his actions. The shooter's name was Frank Candor. Frank had recently lost his job as a forklift operator at a local warehouse. He was single with no kids. He was one of two children in a relatively good family who had lived in our community for the past ten years. His letter stated he was unhappy with many things that seemed minor to me: problems with his recent employer; loneliness; and his life had no meaning. Apparently, these issues had been weighing heavily on Frank. The warehouse where he worked was owned by the same owner of the grocery store. Maybe this act was some kind of revenge against the storeowner.

During this entire ordeal, I thought about the victims. None of these grocery store patrons or workers even knew Frank. They were complete strangers to Frank. Why would he kill perfect strangers who had not harmed him in any way?

As I wrestled with these questions, I could not find answers. I could not rationalize why this tragedy occurred. The bigger question that was echoing through my mind was Martha Main's question: "Mayor, what is Trial Town going to do to prevent tragedies like this one?"

What could Trial Town do to prevent tragedies like this from happening in the future? Should we post guards at all merchants? Should we outlaw weapons like the one used in this crime to prevent other such crimes? Should we outlaw weapons in Trial Town altogether to prevent gun crimes? Should all public places have metal detectors at all major entryways?

I hardly had time to think about any of these questions before Martha caught me as I was leaving my office at City Hall. I had to give her an interview.

After filling Martha in on most of the data associated with the crime, she asked the question I dreaded the most. "Mayor, what is Trial Town going to do to prevent tragedies like this one?"

"Martha, we have to do something. There's simply no way that we can tolerate crimes like this one in the future. I have several ideas that I need to discuss with the city council before I commit to any actions."

Martha persisted. "Mayor, are you at least going to consider banning weapons like the one used in this crime?"

"Weapon bans are certainly an option we'll consider."

"With all due respect, Mayor, I think weapon bans deserve much more than consideration. What will it take before you take this problem seriously?"

I was a little taken off guard and was somewhat choked up and angry at the same time. "Martha, let me assure you that I take this event very seriously. We'll do what we can to prevent such a tragedy from ever occurring again."

We convened a special city council meeting to discuss ideas about how we could prevent this type of crime from ever occurring again. With the tragedy fresh in our minds, we were on a mission to do whatever we could. We passed sweeping laws that included:

• restricting guns throughout Trial Town's city limits, except for our police force and military;

• making it mandatory for all merchants and public places to post signage that announced that they were gun-free zones; and

• a buy-back program for all guns that were currently in circulation.

We named our new changes the Stop Guns program. We had only one city council member vote no. Of course the 'no' vote was Paul Fredrick. Paul indicated he felt the Stop Guns program was an assault on our personal liberty and freedom.

We did get a lot of push back from many gun owners who claimed that they needed their guns for self-protection, hunting, and every other excuse under the sun. I could not see any reason why any citizen in Trial Town needed a gun. The majority of citizens and the city council agreed with me.

The victims' families told me after our actions, they were quite pleased with the Stop Guns program. They felt maybe their family members who died in the tragedy had at least died for a reason and future lives would be saved.

Chief Boston was a stickler about ensuring that merchants posted the proper signage and that we collected all the guns that had been registered in

Trial Town. A few guns were reported as lost or stolen, but we felt we'd collected all of the guns that could be collected.

I felt very good about the efforts that we made to prevent a crime like the one that happened at Anderson's Grocery Store from ever happening again.

It was almost been a year since the Stop Guns program had been in force. I was fast asleep at 1 a.m. on a Saturday morning when my home phone rang. I was tempted to ignore it but decided to answer. There was no mistaking the voice on the other end of the line. It was Chief Boston. "Boss, we have had another shooting incident at the Short Branch Liquor Store."

I was surprised. "Craig, did anyone die?"

"The cashier was killed."

"Did you catch the guy who committed the crime?"

"No. We haven't caught the shooter at this point. The store did have a camera and we will review the video to see what happened. I hope that we can ID the perpetrator. We were notified of the problem with the activation of the silent alarm from the liquor store but weren't able to get to the store in time to catch the guy."

The next morning I got more information from Chief Boston. Apparently, the liquor store was robbed. Two thousand dollars was taken from the register along with some bottles of hard liquor. We still had no good leads even with the camera footage as the perpetrator was wearing a ski mask and there were no telltale signs of the perpetrator.

Over the next year, there were other crimes similar to the liquor store robbery. Most did not end with a fatality but there were injuries and loss of money. Since passing the Stop Guns program, it seemed like crime had increased in general, with a marked increase in gun crime. I know this sounds bad, but I felt better about these crimes. They were much less tragic than the event in the grocery store. I certainly felt for the merchants who lost money and the lives that were lost, but at least I could understand the motives for these robberies. What happened in the grocery store had just seemed senseless.

It had now been two years since the Stop Guns program was passed. I was eating lunch at Pirate's Cove when I got a call from Chief Boston on my cell phone. The chief reported another shocking gun crime. Apparently, a gunman had walked into the Trial Town Elementary School and shot several students in the first grade classroom. The gunman also shot the first grade teacher and the school principal and then killed himself. The Chief did not know the identity of the shooter or his motive when he called.

My heart sank. I felt even worse about this tragedy than I did about the grocery store shooting two years earlier. I immediately paid my bill and left Pirate's Cove to join Chief Boston at Trial Town Elementary School.

Words cannot describe the crime scene at the Trial Town Elementary School. I could only imagine the horror that the victims felt. A gunman shooting at little kids? These children had only been on this planet for six years and some nutcase decided to kill them… along with a teacher, a principal and himself. If these people are suicidal, why can't they just kill themselves? Why in the world are these people killing innocent people…. especially six-year-old kids?

We went through the typical commotion with reporters and carried out our investigation. It was determined that the gunman was a 20-year-old male named Jimmy Porter. Jimmy was apparently still living with his parents. He had been on medication for bi-polar disorder and his parents indicated that Jimmy would not take his medication occasionally and could get quite depressed. They both claimed they had no idea he was capable of killing. Let alone capable of a mass shooting like the one that occurred at Trial Town Elementary School. When asked how Jimmy got the gun for his shooting spree, the parents claimed they had no idea Jimmy even had a gun. In our investigation, we found that Jimmy obtained the gun from a dealer in Capital City, where it was still legal to sell guns to citizens.

I had to think about this situation a little more. I could not imagine doing more to control guns in Trial Town. We had banned guns. In yet, the bad guys were still getting their hands on guns. The gun bans were only keeping guns out of the hands of storeowners and others. Most of the people who would use guns responsibly were not allowed to use guns. We had plastered 'gun-free zone' signs all over Trial Town; these signs were obviously ignored by the bad guys. In fact, I think the gun-free-zone signs probably assured any criminal that the place they raided would be unprotected.

I thought, "Maybe we didn't go far enough. Maybe we could have metal detectors at all public places and staff these metal detectors with trained security guards. It would be a large expense, but I just couldn't get the images of those dead children out of my mind. We have to do whatever it takes to prevent these things from happening ever again."

I then proposed a program to the city council to put metal detectors at the main entrance to any public facility. The city council was okay with putting metal detectors at the entrance to any publicly owned buildings, but was reluctant to force private merchants to install metal detectors and have them manned by security guards unless they consented. The city council approved a Detect Guns program, to pay $100 million per year to prevent guns from ever entering our government-owned institutions. If private merchants wanted the metal detectors and security guards, they would have to pay for these services on their own. Many merchants were upset with us as they felt they could have provided this security themselves if the city had not banned guns. I could not tolerate having any guns in Trial Town. I was convinced that this new initiative would solve the problem.

We made it another two years without an incident with any of the public places that had metal detectors and security guards. There was still the occasional liquor store robbery, but no gun incident came close to the previous tragedies at the elementary school and the grocery store. The cost of the security was a little higher than we anticipated. I felt the added cost was worth it.

It was a Friday night, about 8:00 p.m., when I got a call on my cell phone. I quickly noticed the number on my phone. It was Chief Boston. "Mayor, you won't believe this. We have had a major tragedy at the Movietown Theatre."

"Craig, what happened?"

"A gunman shot ten people; two have been pronounced dead and the others have been rushed to the local hospital."

"Craig, are you kidding me? Did the security guard let a gunman through the metal detector?"

The Chief responded, "Mayor, there was a long line in front of the metal detector and the security guard was doing a thorough job of checking people entering the theatre. The gunman shot folks who were waiting in the long line."

I was shocked. "Didn't the security guard do anything to stop the gunman?"

The Chief responded, "Mayor, we decided we would not arm the security guards as we wanted to eliminate any source of guns near a public building. The security guard was one of the people shot and killed."

We got through all of the typical investigation and press briefings. It was not a lot different from the other shootings. I felt literally helpless as the city leader to be able to do anything about gun violence in Trial Town. It seemed like gun crimes had actually increased after we had eliminated guns from our community. How could this be? We had done all that we could possibly do and the problem had grown worse.

One of Trial Town's merchants, Doug Stallworth, had been quite upset when we started the Stop Guns program. Doug owns a sporting goods store in Trial Town and he lost a lot of revenue in gun sales when we passed the Stop Guns program. I decided to set up a meeting with him to get his input on the situation.

I met Doug at my usual place, Pirate's Cove restaurant. Doug was openly opposed to the Stop Guns program and called me some ugly names after I had initially proposed the plan. I was a little concerned about this meeting. However, I felt I needed to hear his perspective.

I started our conversation. "Thanks, Doug, for meeting with me."

"Mayor, I want to apologize for the names I called you a while back. I was upset about the Stop Guns initiative. I'm still upset about that law, but I shouldn't have called you the things I did."

"Doug, I accept your apology. In fact, I know it's been almost five years now, but I would like to hear your objections to the Stop Guns law."

"My main concern at the time was my loss in revenue from gun sales, among other things. I guess this was rather selfish."

I tried to change the direction of the conversation a little. "Doug, my main concerns don't necessarily involve your business."

"What do you want to discuss then?"

"I want to talk about the crime problem we seem to have since the Stop Guns initiative."

"Mayor, I understand that you have attempted to make owning or using a gun completely illegal in Trial Town. Something you don't seem to understand is that guns are just as much a deterrent to crime as they are a cause of crime."

"Doug, don't you agree that if we rid Trial Town of guns altogether, there will be less gun crime?"

Doug smiled. "All you do when you outlaw guns is prevent law-abiding citizens from buying and owning guns. Criminals will always find ways to get whatever they need to commit whatever crime they have in mind. If you keep merchants, homeowners and all of the rest of the good guys from owning guns, many criminals feel there will be no resistance. It doesn't matter if it's a liquor store thief or some nutcase who wants to go on a shooting spree. If they know the place they are attacking won't be defended, they feel free to do what they want."

"Doug, do you mean that we should arm teachers, grocery store clerks and city hall workers?"

"I can't speak for those people. I can tell you that if I were a teacher, I would want to be able to defend myself and be able to defend all of those defenseless children."

I then had a vision of a schoolteacher having a shootout with some armed criminal. What was this... the Wild West? "Doug, I don't think a shootout between a teacher and a gunman adds much safety for kids in our schools."

"I agree that a shootout is a bad situation. I'm saying that if teachers are allowed to have guns, a shooter will be less likely to believe that he or she can attack defenseless victims."

"What if we arm the security guards who staff our metal detectors?"

Doug smiled. "Mayor, I have seen those security guards. No offense, but I'd feel more uneasy about them having a gun than me having a gun."

"So what do you suggest?"

Doug seemed eager to reply. "After the Stop Guns initiative, I've given this issue a lot of thought. You want to have guns in the hands of the good guys and you want to make it as hard as possible for the bad guys to obtain guns."

I smiled. "How can you tell the good guys from the bad guys? Do you have some special mind-reading device?"

Doug laughed. "No, I don't have a mind-reading device. I acknowledge there's no foolproof method of separating good guys from bad guys. However, we can only sell guns to people who don't have a violent criminal record or a history of mental illness."

I played devil's advocate. "What if someone has a mental illness that is not diagnosed or publicly known?"

"Like I said, the program isn't foolproof. I for one feel having most of the good guys armed is a much larger deterrent than trying to keep all potential criminals from getting guns. Even if I don't sell criminals or mentally ill people guns, they'll figure out ways to get them. You've seen this happen in Trial Town over the past five years."

After my meeting with Doug, I was convinced that we had gone the wrong direction in Trial Town. We had attempted to eliminate guns from our society, which we thought would eliminate gun violence. Instead, we seem to have emboldened criminals to attack defenseless merchants, homeowners and institutions with illegally obtained guns.

I then proposed to the city council that we abolish the Stop Guns and Detect Guns initiative. I further proposed that we replace these initiatives with security checks for those who purchase guns and try as hard as we can to keep guns out of the hands of the 'bad guys.' I also felt we should encourage merchants to remove the 'gun-free zone' signs that were required as part of the Stop Guns program. In place of the 'gun-free zone' signs, I advocated they put up signs that advertised they might be armed.

When I presented these ideas to the city council, half of our council members insisted that we should further restrict guns in our community. The vote to abolish the gun control laws was 3-3. I then cast the tie-breaking vote to complete the abolishment of our gun control laws.

After we abolished our gun control laws, we fewer issues with armed robberies and other smaller crimes. There were no mass shootings. A large number of citizens decided to own guns for their self-protection. My sense was that close to 30% of the merchants and other citizens were armed in their places of work or home. I also noticed that several merchants took my advice and put up signs on the front of their establishments. These signs read, *'In order to provide protection of our patrons, property and employees, we incorporate video camera footage and may be armed.'* Each sign was slightly different, but they all sent a clear message that the building occupants may own a weapon.

I was uneasy when we first abolished our gun control laws. I personally have never felt comfortable around guns, and so I felt these guns were the cause of most of our violence problems. After five years without our gun control laws, I now feel more comfortable that the right people own guns and are the best deterrent we have against further gun violence.

Real World Examples

The ownership of guns in the United States was established as a right in the Second Amendment to the constitution.

Since the time of the founding of the US, when this amendment was enacted, several people have questioned this right. Some have claimed that citizen gun ownership was established for colonies to protect themselves from invasions from foreign armies who also have guns. There is no way we could defend ourselves against a tyrannical government that has access to very powerful weapons. Therefore, the Second Amendment is outdated and not applicable in today's climate of gun violence.

In the light of many recent tragedies very similar to the ones mentioned in Trial Town, many advocates of gun control have been successful in passing background check laws, illegalization of assault weapons, and implementation of many gun-free-zones. Guns are not allowed on airplanes, schools, many public buildings, malls and theatres. In many cases, enforcement of gun-free-zones is the honor system. Metal detectors along with unarmed security guards are used in our airports.

A hard reality is no amount of security that can guarantee complete safety. When institutions try to eliminate guns from their premises, the cost of such security can be infinite and unaffordable in the end. Attempts to create gun-free-zones are actually advertisements to most bad guys that these places are unprotected. The most cost-effective way to ensure the best possible security is to allow responsible citizens to carry arms to protect themselves, their property and their families.

Background checks, gun safety training, and other restrictions are certainly understandable as long as the good guys are not disadvantaged with gun control laws.

13 CLOSE THOSE BORDERS

"A nation that cannot control its borders is not a nation."
— Ronald Reagan

Trial Town did not start with its current population of 100,000 people. Just five people settled in this location originally. The community then grew as people immigrated from all over the land. Over 200 years we have grown through normal population growth and immigration to the 100,000 citizens that we have today. The good news is that Trial Town is a very attractive place to live. We have a very well developed economy, industry, education system, healthcare system, recreation, and an ethical government. The bad news is that it appeared too many outsiders wanted to come to Trial Town.

Early in Trial Town's history, when we had a population of 50,000 citizens, the immigration situation prompted our city council to take up the issue of immigration control. The city felt it needed to establish quotas that would limit the number of immigrants Trial Town would accept to 1% of the current Trial Town population. At that time, that would mean 500 immigrants per year. At our current population, this law restricts our annual immigrant population to 1,000. Unfortunately, many more immigrants want to move to Trial Town.

About twenty years ago, we noticed a trend of immigrants coming to Trial Town and bypassing the formal application process to enter our town.

At the time, we suspected that about 500 immigrants per year were entering Trial Town without going through our formal application system. These immigrants are called "undocumented immigrants". Some folks call them "illegal aliens."

Ten years ago, Trial Town passed a law to further reduce quotas of immigrants as the city council felt that there were still too many immigrants. Instead of reducing overall immigration, the undocumented immigrant migration to Trial Town increased to an estimated 1,000 people per year.

Five years ago, Trial Town felt there were too many immigrants living illegally, with no formal citizenship, in our town. We then passed a law to accept all of these immigrants legally in order to eliminate the need for these folks to live as law-breakers. The law was called the Immigrant Acceptance Law. Some people called this 'amnesty,' as we were excusing illegal immigration. When this law was passed, 4,000 immigrants were formally accepted as legal citizens of Trial Town.

That brings us to our current situation. Even though we have tried to enforce strict immigrant control, we have several people migrating from Southern Town, which is located only 500 miles from Trial Town. Southern Town has a large population of folks who live in poverty. They see Trial Town as a great place to move their family. These immigrants believe they can find work and have a better life for their family. At present, we feel there are once again 4,000 undocumented immigrants living in Trial Town, even though we have established a limit of 0.5% in documented immigrants from all communities outside of Trial Town.

I decided to set up a special city council meeting to discuss this problem with council members and try to come up with a fix to this problem for the last time. I called our meeting to order, briefly outlined the history of the problem, and then opened up the floor for discussion.

Paul Fredrick was the first to speak. "Mayor, I think that we need to build a fence and staff that fence with guards to shut down the illegal immigration altogether."

Sally Hatfield, a city council member who usually opposed Paul, was thinking about an opportunity for building her voting base by befriending the undocumented immigrants and by being soft on the immigration issue. "Paul, what a hostile approach to immigration. I personally like these immigrants. Building a fence is a purely racist approach in an attempt to control Trial Town's population. I think you just don't like Southern Towner's. After all, our ancestors were all immigrants at one point in Trial Town's history."

I then interjected. "Sally, Paul proposed a fence. What do you propose as a solution to our undocumented immigrant problem?"

Sally was caught a little off guard. "I think that we should pass another

Acceptance Law that makes any current undocumented immigrant legal and keeps these folks from operating outside of the law."

Paul immediately reacted. "All we'd do with another Acceptance Law is encourage more undocumented immigrants to migrate into Trial Town, making our problem worse. Sally, your motives are quite transparent. I know that you almost received 80% of the vote from the folks who moved from Southern Town in your most recent election. You're just trying to pad your votes for the next city council election."

After these remarks I had to weigh in. "Okay, okay, you both need to just settle down. I don't think we're making much headway in solving this problem. Let me restate the problem. We established a quota of 1% of our population twenty years ago. We then reduced this quota to 0.5% ten years ago. Despite these limitations, it seems our undocumented immigrant problem gets worse. We did pass an Acceptance Law five years ago only to find that we are in a similar situation today."

Paul responded, "Mayor, I'm telling you, if we build a big fence and put our military on the fence, we'll eliminate the undocumented immigrant problem in Trial Town. After the fence is built, we can then talk about passing another Acceptance Law for those who currently live in Trial Town."

A local union steward, Jack Tate, from the Trial Town Paper Mill wanted to speak. I called on Jack. "Jack, I recognize you to speak. Please join our discussion."

"Mayor, council members, I'd like to endorse Paul's proposal for constructing a fence around Trial Town. I believe that illegal aliens have severely hampered our ability to earn a living wage here in Trial Town. These people come into our town and won't join unions. They tend to work for much less than what we need to earn a decent living. I also suspect many of them get paid under the table, so they don't pay taxes to Trial Town."

At this point Sally realized that she had a political dilemma. Even though she received a large vote from Southern Town immigrants, she also received a large vote from the union members in Trial Town. Sally immediately responded to Jack's statement. "I agree with Jack. If we legalize the current undocumented immigrants, they would be eligible to join unions and earn similar wages. Therefore they wouldn't diminish the living wage that Jack is referring to."

Jack seemed to be satisfied with Sally's response and sat down.

Paul Fredrick then spoke up again. "There are many other problems associated with simply allowing immigrants to flood into Trial Town unchecked. These folks take advantage of Trial Town's entitlement programs like welfare, our public education system, free healthcare and other services that are paid for by Trial Town taxpayers. We really need to build and reinforce a fence." Paul then made a motion. "I move that we build a fence and reinforce this fence with an expansion of our military. This action should not cost more than $50 million per year."

Jerry Pate quickly spoke up. "I second the motion."

I then stated, "It has been moved and seconded that we build a fence and staff it with our military. It is further moved that Trial Town invest up to $50 million per year to enforce Trial Town's borders in order to prevent additional undocumented immigrants from entering Trial Town. Is there any discussion?"

Sally Hatfield spoke up. "It looks like you all may go ahead with this crazy fence idea. I'd like to offer a simple amendment to Paul's motion. I think that we should pass another Acceptance Law that makes any undocumented immigrants legal once the fence has been completed."

Frank Stetson offered, "I second Sally's motion to amend Paul's original motion."

I then took a deep breath and restated the motion. "It has been moved and seconded to build a fence, staff it with our military for up to $50 million per year and we institute an Acceptance Law that legalizes any undocumented immigrants who live in Trial Town once the fence is constructed. Is there any discussion?"

All council members seemed to like the motion and so there was no further discussion.

I asked for the vote. "All in favor of the motion raise your hand." All council members raised their hand. I then closed out the issue. "It appears that the motion on the floor passed with a 6-0 vote and so we will implement this action over the next year. Thank you, council members, for engaging in this discussion. I think we've made a good decision on controlling our illegal immigration problem."

Over the next year, we implemented all of the initiatives that the council had recommended. We engaged many workers from within and outside of Trial Town to construct a fence that was twenty feet high and extended one hundred miles around the perimeter of our town. There were seven entry points in the fence that were patrolled 24-hours per day. We did get a few immigrants penetrating our fence but for the most part, immigration rates for both legal and illegal immigrants seemed to level off at 1%. This was more than our established quota of 0.5%, but quite manageable nonetheless. We then legalized the undocumented immigrants that had entered Trial Town.

I was quite happy with our solution to our immigrant problem until I was confronted by Sammy Penbrook, our tax assessor. Apparently, we were experiencing some financial problems. Sammy wanted to show me some financial charts and tables so he invited me into the city hall conference room.

I entered the conference room and started our conversation. "Sammy, what do you have for me?"

Sammy showed me a slide that showed a chart.

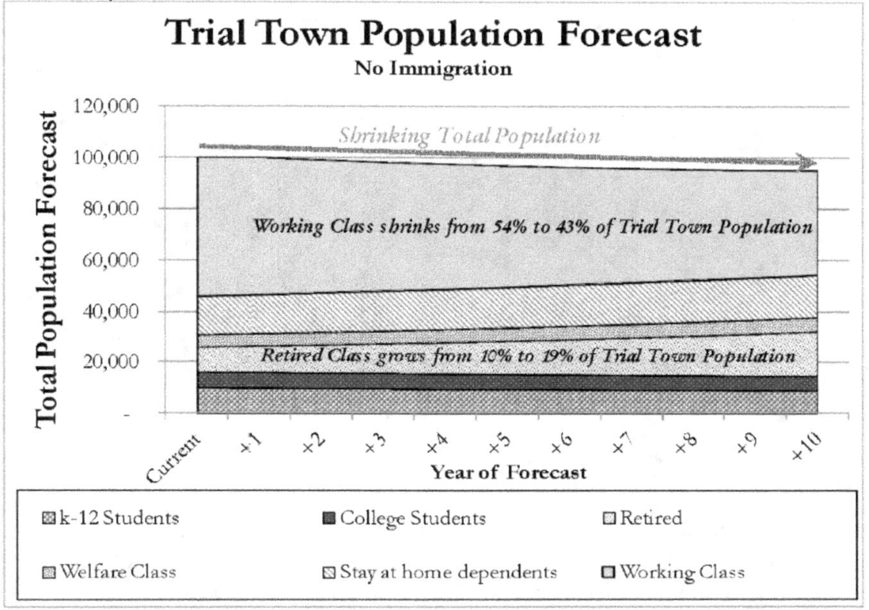

Sammy then started talking. "Mayor, this chart shows a 10-year forecast of Trial Town's population over the next ten years."

"Sammy, I noticed that the title to your chart says 'No Immigration.' What does immigration have to do with our retirement program?"

Sammy smiled. "I'm glad you asked, Mayor. Before I talk about immigration, I want to give you a better understanding of the current demographics in Trial Town that are causing this funding shortfall.

It turns out that we have a 'baby boomer' generation that's going to be retiring over the next ten years. This means that the retired portion of our population will increase from 10% to 19% of our population over the next ten years. This is happening while our working class will decrease from 54% to 43% over the same time."

I was confused. "So what, Sammy? Why is that a problem?"

Sammy then showed me a second chart.

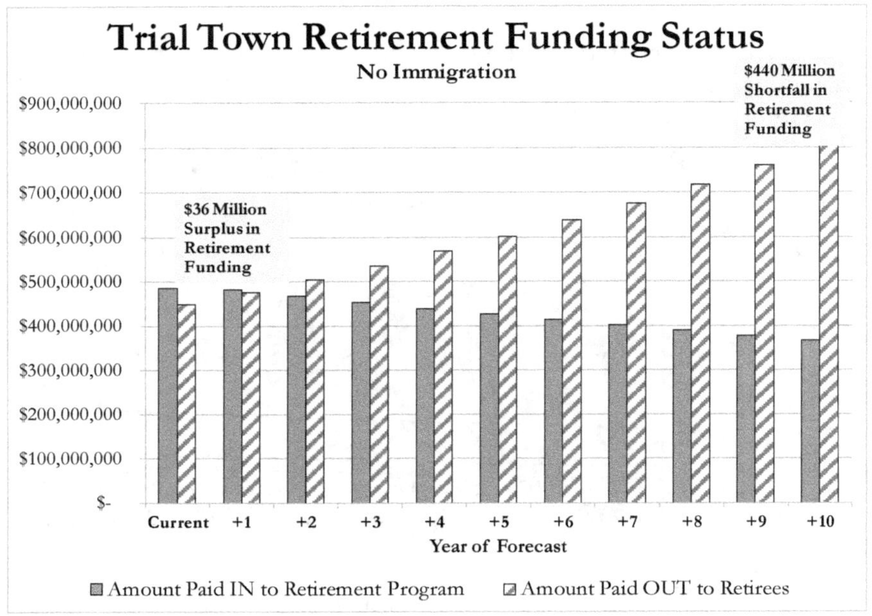

Sammy continued. "The working class folks pay taxes into Trial Town. These taxes go to pay for all of Trial Town's services, including our retirement programs for retirees. When Trial Town's working class drops relative to our retired population, there are less tax revenues to pay for retirement programs as well as other government services."

"Okay, okay, I get it. Again, what does immigration have to do with our retirement financial shortfall?"

Sammy then showed another chart.

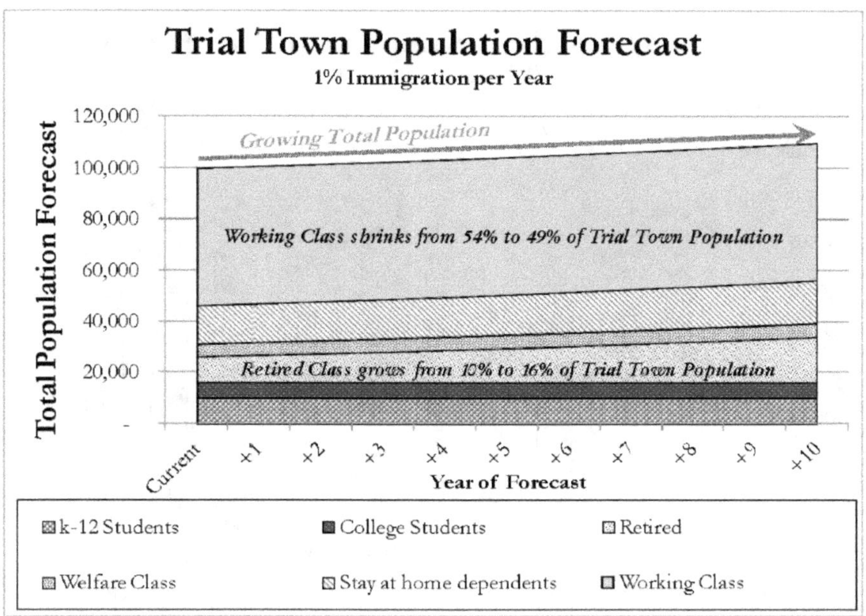

Sammy said, "Remember last year you asked me to see how immigration impacted our budget?"

"Yes, I remember. I personally felt immigration, legal or illegal, would stress our economy."

Sammy smiled. "Here's the chart that shows the impact on our retirement program with only 1% immigration. This is the rate of immigration that we have currently."

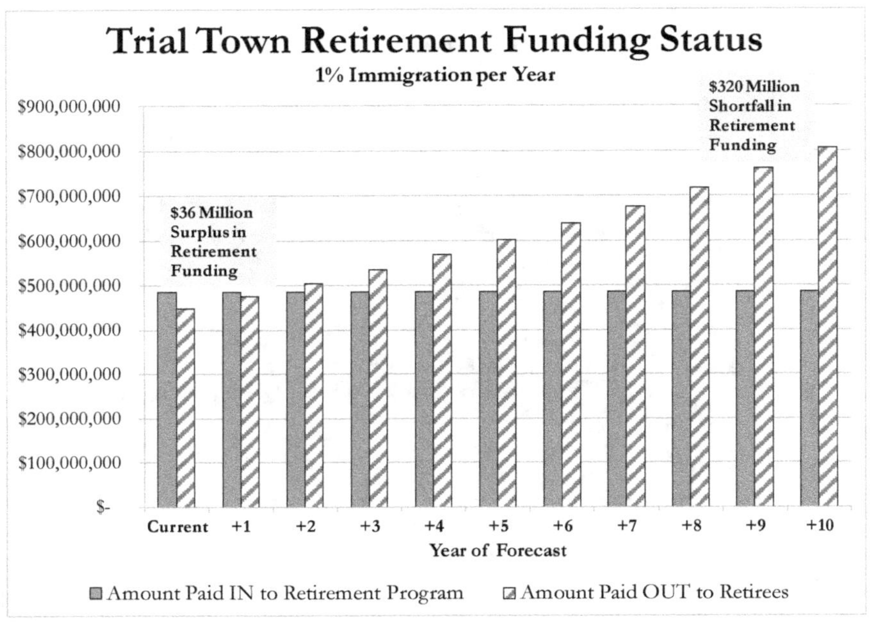

I was amazed. "Wow! With 1% immigration, our retirement funding problem decreases from $440 million per year to losses of $320 million per year. This isn't what I'd have guessed. Why is this true?"

"Most immigrants are young families. These migrating families tend to increase the working class population. As I mentioned before, working class folks pay taxes, helping us improve our financial situation."

"That may be, Sammy, but these folks also have school-aged children who increase the cost of our education system."

Sammy admitted, "You're right Mayor. Even so, immigrants who are working will improve our financial situation. They'll be especially beneficial to support the retirement of our baby boomers."

I then asked, "Sammy, if 1% immigration reduces our retirement funding problem, what level of immigration would eliminate our retirement funding problem?"

Sammy smiled. "I knew you'd ask that question. I've already prepared a chart."

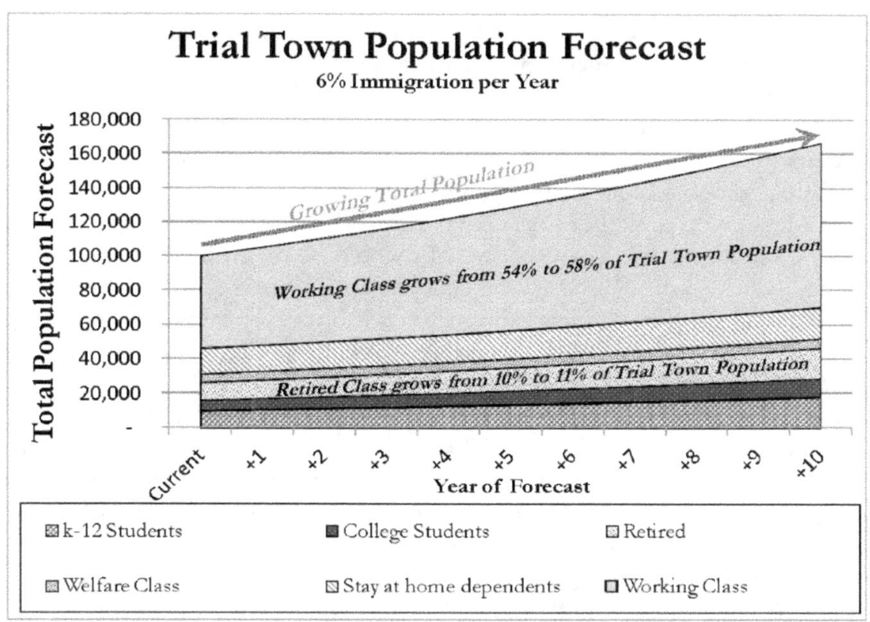

After I looked at the chart, I freaked out a little. "Sammy! How can Trial Town support this high a growth rate? In ten years we'll have grown from 100,000 people to over 160,000 people."

Sammy then calmly showed me another chart.

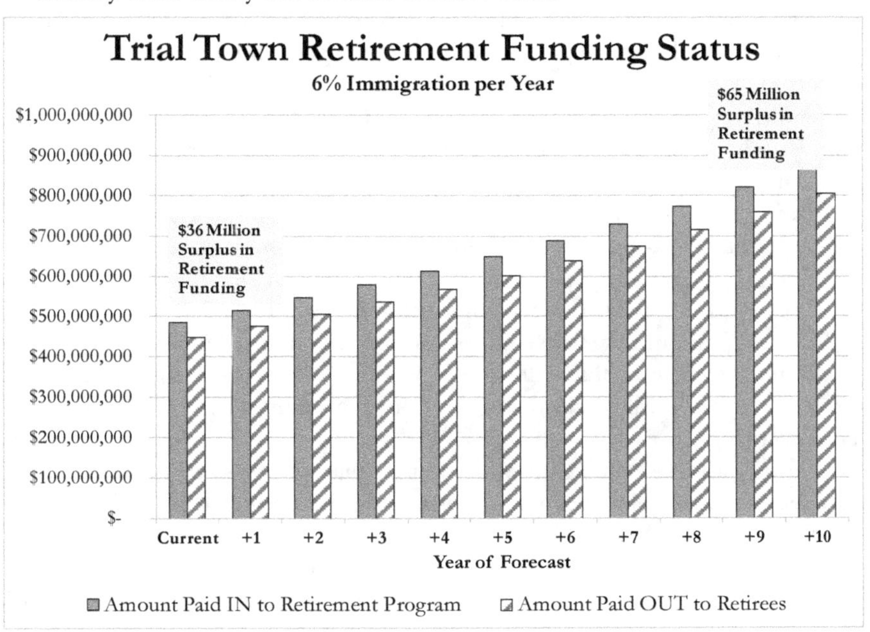

Sammy stated, "If immigration were to increase to 6%, we could create a surplus in our retirement program along with all of our government programs."

I then played devil's advocate. "If we allowed 6% immigration, we would grow to a population of close to 170,000 in ten years. Won't this require additional costs in all of our government services?"

"Mayor, you're right. However, all of these services will be paid for by a strong working class. The other benefit would be that the students who are being educated in our schools, colleges and trade schools will be well prepared to support the new retirement class once they join the workforce."

I was skeptical. "No offense, Sammy, but I just don't know if I believe any of your numbers."

"Mayor, we've tested this theory by reviewing budgets and immigration numbers for the past 20 years. What we've found is that we need to keep our working class at or above 53% in order to fund the government programs we currently have in place. Immigration could be kept at 5%, but I believe Trial Town has plenty of capacity to grow way above our current population. A 6% immigration rate is not only sustainable but can keep Trial Town financially viable into the future."

I then decided to have Sammy present his charts and tables at our next city council meeting.

I started the meeting. "Council members, I believe we didn't fully understand our financial situation, when we decided to build our fence and limit immigration to 1%. Sammy Penbrook has some charts that he'd like to present to shed some light on our immigration and retirement program situation."

Sammy gave the city council members the same presentation he gave me. I recognized many of the questions asked by our council members as the same questions that I had posed to Sammy in the conference room.

Paul Fredrick then spoke up. "Mayor, are you saying that we have wasted money and time building and staffing our fence to keep illegal aliens out?"

I responded, "Paul, I don't think the fence is a bad idea. However, I do believe we should increase the quotas we had established for legal immigrants. I believe this will greatly decrease the stress on the fence in the near term and will help us solve our retirement program's financial situation."

Sammy added, "One caution is that immigrants need to be workers and not retirees or welfare recipients. Otherwise the predicted financial benefits won't be realized."

Sally Hatfield then saw an opportunity to take a leadership position. "I move that Trial Town increases its quota of immigrants from 0.5% to 6%."

Frank Stetson spoke, "I second Sally's motion."

I then stated, "It's been moved and seconded that we increase our immigration quota from 0.5% of Trial Town's current population to 6% of Trial Town's current population. Is there any discussion?"

Paul Fredrick then spoke up. "In keeping with Sammy's recommendation, I propose to amend Sally's motion to include restrictions on the types of immigrants we allow into Trial Town. Immigrants must be working class and not be eligible for retirement or welfare benefits for a period of ten years."

Jerry Pate spoke up. "I second Paul's amendment to Sally's motion."

I then stated, "It has been moved and seconded that Trial Town increase its immigration limits from 0.5% to 6% of Trial Town's current population. As a condition of this increase, it's further moved that restrictions be placed on immigrants to restrict retirement and welfare benefits for a period of ten years. Is there any discussion?"

Once again, the city council seemed to be satisfied with the modified motion and voted 6-0 to pass our new immigration law.

We increased our staff in the immigration department to accommodate the increase in our immigration limits. However, Trial Town's cost was reduced once we reduced our staff defending the fence that surrounded Trial Town.

Five years later, we saw financial benefits that were very close to what Sammy had predicted. Our government programs were fully funded with a substantial surplus. The immigrants who came to Trial Town became contributing members of Trial Town's economy almost immediately. Some immigrants entered the cleaning work force, some in construction, some in our paper industry, some in farming and some started their own businesses that employed other Trial Town citizens. Immigrants came from many other areas than Southern Town. Since these immigrants could enter Trial Town legally, undocumented immigrants were non-existent. The immigration rate tended to average a little over 5%.

Our town grew. Our retirees were taken care of and our schools were stronger than ever. I'm so glad Sammy educated me on the benefits of immigration and how higher immigration rates ultimately helped Trial Town eliminate its retirement program funding problems.

Real World Examples

The United States passed the Emergency Quota Act in 1921 that limited immigrants to 3% of individual nationalities within the country. In other words, if the US had 100,000 Germans, German immigrants were limited to 3,000 in any single year. In 1952, the US updated its immigration policy to restrict the total amount of immigrants to the US regardless of nationality. In 2013, the legal limit of immigrants to the US was 675,000 per year. This is effectively 1.8% of the United States' current population. Our total population growth in the United States is roughly 1% per year even with 1.8% legal immigration rate. It is estimated that close to 15 million undocumented immigrants exist in the United States. The US also has a baby boomer population that will be retiring between 2013 and 2025, resulting in a deficit of close to $70 trillion in funding for Social Security.

Conservative politicians seem to favor reinforcing our borders to prevent illegal immigrants and other non-desirable folks from entering the US. Liberal politicians seem to want to soften any restrictions on immigration or border control.

Just like Trial Town, the US could improve its legal immigration volumes to 5%, allowing immigrants to enter our country legally and reducing the stress on our border situation. Border security should still be enforced. There are many people crossing the border into the US who are international criminals. As part of the immigration policy, the US should continue to have working requirements on immigrants and not allow people to migrate to the US who simply want a free ride with medical, welfare, retirement, food stamp or other social entitlement programs.

In November 2014, President Obama passed an Executive Order in an attempt to side-step congress and grant legal status to approximately 5,000,000 illegal immigrants. Just prior to this announcement, several refugees from Latin America were being detained in holding areas after being allowed to cross the border without resistance. Most of these refugees were children. Just prior to this large refugee move, President Obama announced that he would not deport any family who had children living in the U.S. Unfortunately, many of these refugees were not able to work to offer any financial benefit as was highlighted in the Trial Town story.

The U.S. needs to establish firm immigration policies and laws and enforce these laws. It is my personal opinion that we need to at least double our current immigration quotas and make it easier to migrate to the U.S. Contrary to those who fear excess job competition, many immigrants take jobs Americans don't want; and they contribute to a robust service economy.

14 A LIVING WAGE

"We cannot legislate prosperity. When we increase minimum wages by legislative fiat, we kill jobs."
— John Stossel

Trial Town was doing quite well with its economy and our government was streamlined. Our unemployment rate had dropped down to almost 3%. This was almost unheard of as our unemployment rate was usually 5%, during the best of times. Things were going so well I set up a special city council meeting to brag about how well things were going in Trial Town. During my presentation, the city council members and I had great cause for celebration. As with all of our city council meetings, this meeting was open to the public. After I completed my presentation, I opened up the floor for public comment.

Barbara Stanton stepped up to the podium and began her talk. "Mayor, it seems like things are going great for Trial Town and for most of Trial Town's citizens. Unfortunately, things are not going well for me. I currently work at Burger Castle for minimum wage. This wage doesn't provide near enough money to support myself and my two children."

I was embarrassed but had to ask, "Barbara, what's the current minimum wage?"

"Mayor, the current minimum wage is $6.00 per hour."

I then asked, "Barbara, what wage do you think would provide a living wage for you and your family?"

Barbara was clearly caught off guard. "I honestly haven't thought about how much I would need to support my family. However, the wage needs to be much more than $6.00 per hour."

I responded, "Barbara, I'll get with our folks internally and see what we can do to increase the minimum wage. I certainly don't want employers in Trial Town to pay folks at a level that doesn't provide a living wage."

After the city council meeting, I set up another meeting with Sammy Penbrook, our tax assessor. Sammy is the best person I know with numbers so I felt he would be the best person to establish a minimum wage.

Sammy started our meeting discussion. "Mayor, how can I help you?"

"Sammy, Barbara Stanton requested that we revisit our current minimum wage of $6.00 per hour. Barbara indicates that she can't make ends meet for herself and her two children with this wage. I believe Trial Town should set a minimum wage that will allow Barbara to pay her bills and have a little left over."

Sammy responded, "Okay, Mayor. It sounds like I need to pay Barbara Stanton a visit."

Sammy set up a meeting with Barbara in order to understand what her hourly wage would need to be in order to support herself and her kids. Barbara was glad to meet with Sammy. She was especially eager since it meant she might be getting a pay increase.

Sammy met Barbara at her apartment, which was located in a poorer part of town. The apartment seemed simple with two bedrooms, one for her kids and one for herself, with a common living space. In the living space, there was a living room and a modest kitchenette with a small dining space.

Sammy started the conversation. "Barbara thanks for meeting with me. I hope you have done the homework I requested over the phone."

Barbara smiled. "Thank you for meeting with me, Sammy. I've completed the homework that you gave me. I've listed all my monthly bills."

Expense	Monthly Amount	
Groceries	$	600
Rent	$	500
Bus Fare	$	125
Gasoline	$	-
Car Insurance	$	-
Car Maintenance	$	-
Clothes	$	100
Cable TV	$	75
Internet	$	70
Hair care	$	50
Entertainment	$	100
Miscelaneous	$	150
Total	**$**	**1,770**

Sammy took the budget Barbara gave him and quickly divided the total monthly amount by 40-hrs per week. Then he divided that result by 4 weeks per month. The resulting hourly wage rate Sammy calculated was $11.06 per hour. Sammy was amazed at the difference between what Barbara made at Burger Castle and her monthly expenses. Barbara only made $6.00 per hour at her current job, resulting in a total monthly income of $960 before any deductions were taken out. If Barbara had two full-time jobs at $6.00 per hour, this would be just enough to pay her meager monthly bills.

Sammy said, "Barbara, I certainly see why our current minimum wage is falling short. If you had two full-time jobs like the one at Burger Castle, you'd just have enough money to pay your bills. Since you're falling so short of paying your bills, how are you making ends meet?"

Barbara hung her head. "Sammy, we've fallen behind on our rent in three cases and have to try to get by with fewer groceries most months. Even though we have cable and internet, this service is cut off repeatedly as I've felt these are low priorities to pay."

"Barbara, I've noticed that you are a single mother. Do you get any alimony or child support to help you with bills?"

"We were never officially married and so it was a challenge to try to collect these payments. Plus my kids' dad isn't making any more than I am with my job. He's out of work most of the time."

"Barbara, I thank you for your time. I'm going to recommend to our Mayor that we increase the minimum wage from $6.00 per hour to $11.00 per hour to help you out. I'm going to also recommend that Trial Town increase the minimum wage by the rate of inflation each year to keep up with the cost of living."

Barbara raised her head and smiled. "Sammy, thank you so much for your help. I really appreciate it."

After the meeting with Barbara, Sammy called me into his office and filled me in on his discussion. "Mayor, I can't see how any person in Barbara's situation can make any less than $11.00 per hour and still make ends meet."

I responded, "It seems like we need to raise our minimum wage in Trial Town to at least $11.00 per hour. Thank you for your research."

I presented Sammy's findings to the city council. The city council voted 4-2 to pass a new minimum wage law to raise the minimum wage to $11.00 and escalate the wage each year based on the rate of inflation. I could not understand how the two heartless council members could have voted no after the story and justification Sammy presented.

Barbara Stanton was present at our city council meeting and she was noticeably happy about the increased minimum wage.

A few months after the minimum wage law passed, I got a call from Barbara Stanton. By the sound of her voice, it was obvious she was crying. "Mayor, I was just laid off from my job at Burger Castle."

I was shocked. "Barbara, why did you get laid off?"

"The manager, Warren Richards, stated that he needed to cut labor costs in order to keep his business going. I was one of the labor costs that he cut. He seemed like a fair man. However, I wondered if I was targeted since I was the one who spoke up to increase Trial Town's minimum wage in the city council meeting?"

I was heartbroken. "Barbara, would it be okay if I talk with Warren about this situation?"

"Mayor, I'd really appreciate that. It couldn't hurt. I thought I was going to be able to pay my bills and now I can't even afford to pay the critical bills."

"I'll talk with Warren. Who knows? Maybe I can get you your job back."

I set up a meeting with Warren at the Burger Castle to talk about the layoff situation and sat down with Warren at one of the tables in the dining area. It was slow at the restaurant as it was 3:00 p.m. and we were between lunch and dinner.

I started the conversation. "Warren thanks for meeting with me today."

"I'm glad to meet with you, Mayor. What can I do for you?"

"Warren, I'll get right to the point. Why did you fire Barbara Stanton?"

"Laying Barbara off was purely a business decision."

"Please describe the details that led to Barbara's dismissal."

"When the minimum wage rose from $6.00 per hour to $11.00 per hour, we had to almost double our prices in order to keep our current staff. At first we tried to just raise our menu prices, believing that our competitors would have to also raise prices as a result of the new law."

"That makes sense to me. So how did that work?"

"I was wrong about our competition. Some of our competitors got creative and were able to keep prices relatively low and still pay their remaining staff the new higher minimum wage. They replaced employees with machines, automating some of their processes."

"Can you give me an example of such a machine?"

"Yes. Pirate's Cove installed an automatic drink pourer. Prior to increase in minimum wage, they had a member of staff pouring drinks. At $6.00 per hour, they couldn't justify purchasing the automatic pouring machine. However, at $11.00 per hour for this low skill position, it made financial sense for Pirate's Cove to buy the machine and lay off the minimum wage employee. "

"Warren, that doesn't make any sense. Pirate's Cove still has to pay for the new machine. This must have resulted in slightly higher costs to their customers."

"Mayor, you're right. In order to pay for the new machine, it was equivalent to paying a staff member $7.50 per hour. Pirate Cove's costs did go up slightly, but these cost increases were not as high as they would be with an $11 per hour employee."

"Let's get back to Burger Castle and Barbara's situation. What happened to Barbara?"

Warren breathed a big sigh and started his explanation. "Barbara was our french-fry person. She was in charge of putting fries in and taking them out during rush hours. This job was only needed four hours per day. However, I was aware that Barbara was trying to raise two kids, so I gave her eight hours per day. When the minimum wage was increased, I had to get creative on cutting costs or we'd have been buried by our competitors. I proposed to Barbara that we cut her hours in half."

I understood why Barbara wouldn't like that deal. "That's a big cut."

"Yes. Even with the minimum wage increasing from $6.00 per hour to $11.00 per hour, her monthly income would drop to $880. Although this was fewer hours, it would result in $80 less per month than she was making at the lower minimum wage."

"Warren I still don't understand why this resulted in firing Barbara."

"Once I proposed the lower hours to Barbara, she got quite upset and said she would do much better on Trial Town's government programs than she could do working for me. With the change in hours, she decided to quit her job. I certainly understand her disappointment but I really didn't know what else to do."

I then felt I needed to educate Warren on Barbara's situation. "Warren, did you know that with the $6.00 per hour wage, Barbara was making half the money she needed to support her family?"

"I would guess that it's almost impossible to support a family at $6.00 per hour. I guess that's why most of our minimum wage earners are high school and college kids trying to make a little extra spending money."

"Warren, would it be at all possible to reinstate Barbara at full-time status? Maybe she could do another job in addition to French Fries."

"Mayor, to be perfectly honest, Barbara wasn't that skilled at any other job. I also don't feel this would be fair to other workers who have demonstrated more ability than Barbara. As it is now, we have combined the french-fry position with the burger grill position so this individual is handling both jobs. I don't think Barbara could handle both positions."

Sadly, I felt I couldn't help Barbara. "Warren thanks for your time today. I feel I have a better understanding of how the minimum wage increase has affected business owners like you."

"Glad I could help, Mayor. If you see Barbara, let her know that I hope she finds a better job."

I was not quite satisfied with Warren's responses. It just sounded like these business owners were greedy and really did not care about people like Barbara.

I decided to meet with James Pennyworth, the owner of our local paper mill. James paid his employees quite well, from what I heard and so I felt he might have some insight on how to pay workers more and still stay competitive. I set up a meeting with James at the Pirate's Cove Restaurant to get his input.

After greetings, I started the conversation. "James, I want to get straight to the point. As you know, Trial Town raised its minimum wage from $6.00 per hour to $11.00 per hour. I then found out that one of the people I tried to help with this effort was laid off from her job. When I met with her boss, I asked him why he fired this worker. He then gave me some song-and-dance about having to cut costs to remain competitive."

"Mayor, nothing you have told me seems out of the ordinary."

I was a little shocked by James' response. "But James, you pay your workers more money. How can you still remain competitive with higher wages?"

James smiled. "Arthur, I pay my workers more money because they are much higher skilled workers than the workers at Burger Castle. If I tried to pay my workers less, they'd just find a job at another paper mill."

"James, how in the world can minimum wage earners afford to live on the low wages they're being paid?"

"My guess is that most folks can't make a living wage at the old or the newly increased minimum wage."

I was confused. "James, are you suggesting that we raise the minimum wage even higher?"

James laughed. "No, no. In fact, I don't think there should be a minimum wage at all."

I was now thoroughly confused. "You've just acknowledged that even the $11.00 per hour won't allow folks to be able to support themselves. If we had no minimum wage, employers like Warren Richards would pay their employees $0.25 per hour."

"Mayor, whatever wage an employer pays and is accepted by employees defines the value of the work being performed. If you increase the minimum wage, you're restricting the ability of an employer to hire staff for very low-skilled work."

"James, are you saying that employers ought to be able to pay as low a wage as they want?"

"Regardless of what level you set the minimum wage, employers will pay the lowest total wages they can."

"James, I don't think that's true. Even though the employee I tried to help lost her job, other employees at Burger Castle are making more money at the same hours they had before."

James smiled. "I'm guessing those employees are probably doing more work for that higher wage."

I then recalled what Warren had told me about his burger grill guy. "You may be right, James. Warren Richards told me his burger grill guy was more skilled than the person I was trying to help. Plus the burger person now had to do burgers and french-fries."

James seemed to understand that I was still a little confused so he added a story. "Mayor, let's say that you have a burger place owner named Jim who sells cheeseburgers for $5.00. He's then told by the government that he needs to double his costs and so he tries to sell his cheeseburgers for $10.00. Unfortunately, the consumer values these cheeseburgers at $5.00. The consumer decides to cook their own burgers at home instead of paying the higher price. Jim then sees his cheeseburger sales drop. Not to mention that Jim's competitors are experiencing the same downturn in their business. Jim's competitors start to innovate to cut costs in an attempt to get their cheeseburger prices back down to $5.00. Let's say that Jim's competitors, with all of the cutting they can manage, can only drop their cheeseburger price to $7.50 and still make an acceptable profit. Even at this lower price, all of the burger joints will see some decline in business. This is part of the law of supply, demand and prices. Higher prices reduce demand."

"Okay, okay. I understand what's going on with these business owners. I guess they're not greedy. Maybe they are just trying to survive. What can I do to help the mother of two children who has to make a living for her family?"

James breathed a big sigh. "Mayor, I'm a business man and understand the nature of business and finances and what it takes to run a business. As for your mother of two children, it sounds like she's in a tough situation. My sense is that increases in the minimum wage won't help her. My personal hope for the mother of two kids is that she takes advantage of Trial Town's welfare payments and tries to seek training to improve her skills so that she can earn a higher wage once her welfare time limit is up."

After my meeting with James, it was apparent that I could not improve Barbara's situation. Barbara did go on Trial Town's welfare program and I did meet with her to encourage her to improve her skills so that she could make a better living for her family. Barbara then did something I thought was very creative. Barbara visited James Pennyworth at the paper mill and asked him what skills she would need to earn more than $15.00 per hour. James was very helpful in pointing Barbara in the direction of upgrading her computer skills. Barbara then took time during her time on welfare to build her work skills.

A year later, I heard a knock on my office door. Then the door opened a crack. Barbara Stanton poked her head in the door and she was smiling.

"Come on in, Barbara. How are you doing?"

Barbara laughed. "I'm doing great, Mayor. I just got a notice from James Pennyworth at the paper mill. He just hired me for an administrative position at the paper mill."

"That's great, Barbara! What's he going to pay you?"

Barbara was still smiling. "He's paying me $17.50 per hour to start."

"That's fantastic."

"Mayor, I just want to thank you for all that you've done. Mostly I want to thank you for your advice to get training to improve my skills. If I had gotten the $11.00 per hour wage a year ago, I'd probably be at that same job at Burger Castle, and would just barely be able to make ends meet. Since I improved my skills, I can now do much better than just make ends meet; I can provide a better life for my kids."

"I'm so happy for you, Barbara. It sounds like the minimum wage increase really didn't help you out much at all."

"The minimum wage increase was certainly a nice gesture. In retrospect, I really needed to improve my skills instead of hope that an employer would pay me more for low-skilled work."

After my conversation with Barbara, I felt my initial inclination to increase the minimum wage rate was probably misguided. I had noticed that in the past year, Trial Town's unemployment rate rose from 3% up to 6%, and more folks were on welfare. I was convinced this unemployment spike could have been a result of raising the minimum wage.

I brought up this topic with the city council in our next meeting. I educated them on my discussions with Barbara, James and Warren. Most of the city council didn't agree with my assertion that the minimum wage may actually be hurting employers and employees in Trial Town.

Paul Fredrick proposed that Trial Town remove the minimum wage completely for a period of one year to see how it affected Trial Town's employment statistics. I was a little leery of eliminating the minimum wage. I had been convinced that the minimum wage didn't provide the benefits that I had hoped; however, no floor on employee compensation seemed like dangerous territory.

After a lot of heated discussion, the city council approved the move to eliminate the minimum wage for a period of one year. The minimum wage would automatically be reinstated at its current level unless the city council voted to keep no minimum wage for Trial Town.

A few months after this decision was enacted, I decided to visit Warren Richards to see how things were going at Burger Castle.

Warren started our discussion. "Mayor, I'm glad to see you again. You didn't seem too happy when you left my restaurant a year ago."

"Warren, I owe you an apology. I spoke with James Pennyworth after my meeting with you and feel I understand the situation you were in after we increased the minimum wage. Today I was wondering how things are going now that Trial Town has completely eliminated the minimum wage?"

"Mayor, we kept a lot of the cost-saving measures and automation in place that we had before and still have some of the higher wage earners doing more work. However, I've hired some high school students to do some low-skilled cleaning in the evenings. We pay these students $5.00 per hour."

"Did you hire as many employees back as you let go more than a year ago?"

"I suppose that we could hire more employees and reduce the compensation of our more skilled workers and eliminate automation that we implemented in the past. Unfortunately, that wouldn't make much practical sense. I had fifty employees prior to the minimum wage increase over a year ago. We then reduced our staff to thirty-five employees and reduced work hours per person. Now that there's no minimum wage, we're back up to forty employees because we still have a lot of the cost efficiency measures, prompted by the initial rise in minimum wage, in place."

After my conversation with Warren, it was apparent that we would never reverse the damage that may have been caused by our initial increase in the minimum wage.

After a year, we re-checked Trial Town's employment numbers. The unemployment rate had dropped from 6% to 4% over the past year and this was certainly encouraging. However, it was not as good as it was before we started messing with the minimum wage. There were also many more high school and college students earning spending money. I also noticed that folks like Barbara, who could not make a living at any entry wage being offered by employers, decided to improve their skills to get higher paying jobs.

When our trial period on the 'no minimum wage' was up, our city council voted 4-2 to eliminate the minimum wage for Trial Town altogether. The lower wages allowed employers the flexibility to hire low-skilled workers; high school and college students had better access to entry level jobs to develop some work skills. Adult workers who had substantial living expenses were forced to upgrade their skills to get better paying jobs. Employers had the flexibility to pay workers based on the value that they provided their customers instead of an arbitrary wage set by the government.

Real World Examples

The minimum wage laws in the United States were initiated in 1938. Since this time, many states and localities have passed their own minimum wage statutes that are above the national minimum wage. Among all industrialized nations, the United States is currently in the middle at $7.25 per hour (2011 rates). Depending on the level of the minimum wage, it may or may not have an impact on employers or employees. If the minimum wage is relatively low, it may not affect the economy at all. If the wage starts to rise into skilled worker pay rates, the story that unfolded in Trial Town will most likely start to impact regional, national and global economies. If an employer in one location is forced to pay higher wages than their competition in other localities, the employer with higher wages will certainly feel a negative impact on their business. This phenomenon has happened in the auto industry globally.

The main reason for politicians to raise the minimum wage is that they advocate that minimum wage earners need to earn a living. However, most minimum wage earners are high school and college students and rarely include a substantial adult population. At the current US minimum wage of $7.25 per hour, a full-time job would result in $1,160 per month or $13,920 per year. Most minimum wage positions are usually part-time so earnings from a single job are less than $13,000 per year. Most individuals would find it difficult to live on these wages. By current standards, a person like Barbara in the Trial Town story would be considered impoverished if she earns less than $19,530 per year. Therefore, Barbara would be living in poverty if she earned a minimum wage in a full-time job in the US. The US minimum wage has never been sufficient to provide a living wage for citizens, even under the most austere conditions.

Welfare recipients in many states will earn between $17,000 per year to $50,000 per year. If adults find themselves in a financial bind, they are more apt to accept welfare benefits than they would be to take a minimum wage job. Most people in minimum wage positions are either supplementing another wage earners income; or they are trying to make spending money, like younger wage earners. The living wage should have nothing to do with the minimum wage.

Throughout the years, the US cannot provide a link between increases in the minimum wage and the elimination of people in poverty. Nor can an increase in the minimum wage be correlated to increases in unemployment. However, behind the scenes, employers are making decisions to hire, fire, and/or automate based on minimum wage requirements and external consumer pressures.

WHAT DOES IT ALL MEAN?

I hope that as you've read the trials of Trial Town, you have learned a few things about what can and cannot work in government. These concepts are not just true in government, but can be true of running a household budget or running a successful business. Unfortunately, many of these concepts are not intuitive to most people. When uniformed and uneducated voters elect a representative government, these concepts tend to be the last things on their mind. Each person showing up to vote has some personal goodie they want from government. Voters rarely think about the ultimate financial and functional consequences.

This book was written to highlight the dire results of many of the currently popular government policies that exist in federal, state and local governments. Many of the concepts attempted in Trial Town are considered great ideas by many people and politicians today. Many of the bad results being experienced by the citizens of Trial Town are being experienced by us here in the United States today. Unfortunately, we do not have a reset button that we can press when we implement bad ideas. However, we can stop or reverse these bad concepts once we are capable of reviewing the positive or negative aspects objectively. Unfortunately, we are also stuck with a polarized electorate that elevates emotional bantering rather than sound logical reason.

A financial demographic table showing the breakdown of various people groups in Trial Town is a very important concept for us all. Financial demographics mean the split of the population in terms of financial status.

Some citizens of Trial Town are retired, some are children incapable of making income and some are poor, requiring almost 100% of their income from the government or private charity. It is important to note that Trial Town required at least 40% of their population to be working and producing wealth in order to pull off even the smallest government funded programs. In the United States in 2009, there were 121 million people working out of a total population of 330 million. This equates to a ratio of 37% working to non-working people. This ratio has increased to 40% recently. Still, a large portion of our population simply does not earn taxable income. These workers are the drivers of any nation's economy. Unfortunately, the government is placing a heavy financial burden on the working class. This heavy burden discourages work. This culture will drive the work force numbers lower and our nation's debt higher. Not to mention we will have baby boomers retiring from 2013 to 2025, leaving a smaller workforce to support these retirees.

The US has a current debt of $18.5 trillion (2015) and growing daily with more and more government programs and spending initiatives being proposed in our nation's capital. It is considered normal budgeting in our nation's capital to spend more than we take in on an annual basis. We need to reverse this trend and start making wiser choices within our government. Otherwise, we will have a debt that may be impossible to rein in at any point.

<u>What Do We Do?</u>

In Trial Town, Mayor Wallaby eventually realized that a moderate-sized government is better than an oversized government. The smaller the government, the less likely that government will adversely affect the free-market engine that drives the economy. Here are my recommendations to get the United States back to an area of prominence on the world stage:

1) Pass a Balanced Budget amendment to our constitution. The only reason the US should borrow funds is to fund a one-time, necessary war or catastrophic event. Debt should not be created by a lack of spending discipline.

2) Make genuine changes in spending/revenue:

   a. Reduce government spending across the board by $1.3 trillion a year
   b. Eliminate current tax loopholes to add $500 billion to tax revenues
   c. Use the resulting $800+ billion per year surplus to pay down debt

3) Simplify the Tax Code to be a flat tax for all

4) Require Congress and the President to read and understand any legislation that is subject to a vote; and require that they be subjected to the same laws they force on citizens

The reality of this kind of fiscal discipline is that we will dramatically cut out redundancy and unneeded government departments. Entitlements will be a temporary safety net and not a permanent source of income for Americans. All of Social Security and Medicare's unfunded liabilities will be fully funded as originally promised. No new government program or spending will be allowed unless projections are realistic. If financial projections are not met as promised, these initiatives should be eliminated or reduced to meet reasonable financial expectations. Currently, spending is simply increased when budgets are ultimately blown by government bureaucrats.

The US constitutional government, as it was designed, offers the best government that this world has ever seen. Budget controls and rules of conflict resolution are put in place to guarantee a much more efficient government than what we have today.

America holds the promise of opportunity, not the promise of entitlement. If our government would get out of the way of opportunity and stop promoting entitlement, we can be a great nation once again.

About the Author

Jeff Schuster grew up in the rural town of Cedaredge, Colorado and now lives with his wife and two children in Highlands Ranch, Colorado. After graduating from Colorado State University in 1987, Jeff worked as an energy efficiency engineer in both the public and private sectors. In 1997, Jeff started his own small engineering and construction firm engaged in completing energy efficiency projects. Jeff has worked in the public and private sector and is well-versed in government and business concerns. These life experiences were the impetus for authoring this book.

www.ingramcontent.com/pod-product-compliance
Lightning Source LLC
Chambersburg PA
CBHW070110290526
45789CB00005B/1987

9781499553499